Tues. 14
leave Frid.
15
Entry 4
map?

ALASTAIR SAWDAY'S
SPECIAL PLACES TO STAY

PORTUGAL

Captivating! An irresistible collection
of fine houses and hotels.

Design:	Caroline King
Maps & Mapping:	Bartholomew Mapping, a division of HarperCollins, Glasgow
Printing:	Canale, Italy
UK Distribution:	Portfolio, Greenford, Middlesex
US Distribution:	The Globe Pequot Press, Guilford, Connecticut

Published in March 2003

Alastair Sawday Publishing Co. Ltd
The Home Farm Stables, Barrow Gurney, Bristol BS48 3RW
Tel: +44 (0)1275 464891 Fax: +44 (0)1275 464887
E-mail: info@specialplacestostay.com Web: www.specialplacestostay.com

The Globe Pequot Press
P. O. Box 480, Guilford, Connecticut 06437, USA
Tel: +1 203 458 4500 Fax: +1 203 458 4601
E-mail: info@globe-pequot.com Web: www.globe-pequot.com

Second edition

ISBN 1-901970-90-6 in the UK
ISBN 0-7627-2553-2 in the US

Printed in Italy

ALASTAIR SAWDAY'S
SPECIAL PLACES TO STAY

PORTUGAL

Captivating! An irresistible collection
of fine houses and hotels.

Guilford
Connecticut, USA

Alastair Sawday Publishing
Bristol, UK

CONTENTS

northern portugal

central portugal

CONTENTS

southern portugal

See the back of the book for:
- Useful vocabulary
- About eating in Portugal & a smattering of recipes
- Wine
- Fado
- What is Alastair Sawday Publishing?
- Alastair Sawday's Special Places to Stay series
- The Little Earth Book • The Little Food Book
- www.specialplacestostay.com
- Booking form • Report form
- Quick reference indices
- Index by property name • Index by place name
- Exchange rates • Explanation of symbols

ACKNOWLEDGEMENTS

Books can come together in strange ways – no stranger, perhaps, than the way our first-ever book was created nine years ago: we walked blithely through the minefield of self-publishing, unaware of the dangers. In this case we knew our stuff and were able to pull it together largely from within the office, with noble efforts – and successes – by Laura Kinch. At the beginning of the project we had the help of Marie Hodges, whose language skills and charm got things off to a flying start; then she fell in love and was lured away, Laura capably steered the project to completion. The great inspection machinery was kept chugging by the unflagging and unflapping Carol Dymond who lives in Portugal; she helped find some magical places for these pages.

Thanks must go, too, to our Production Department – Paul and Rachel, with Julia at the helm. And Jo, Sarah and Roanne have been terrific in support. The whole team has produced a handsome rabbit out of the Portuguese hat.

Series Editor:	Alastair Sawday
Project Co-ordinator:	Laura Kinch
Managing Editor:	Annie Shillito
Production Manager:	Julia Richardson
Web Producer:	Russell Wilkinson
Additional writing:	Jo Boissevain, John Dalton, Carol Dymond, Laura Kinch
Editorial Assistants:	Jo Boissevain, Sarah Bolton, Roanne Finch, Marie Hodges
Production Assistants:	Rachel Coe, Paul Groom
Accounts:	Jenny Purdy
Inspections:	Carol Dymond

A WORD FROM
ALASTAIR SAWDAY

This book is becoming irresistible – I haven't been to Portugal
for ages but an hour or so buried in these pages has unsettled
me. The houses we feature are as exotic, imaginative and
engaging as any in Europe and I am itching to go and see
them again. There is an old world charm and courtesy to the
Portuguese that you will come to expect after staying in a few
of these places. Many of them are filled with fine old furniture
and portraits and have been in the family for hundreds of years.
Others have been hauled, with panache and colour, into this
century. All of them are special in a particular – and charming
    Portuguese way.

Do not confuse Spain and Portugal. Portugal fought for its
independence and any confusion on your part may rankle a
little. They are very separate, very different – and very close.
Thus there is extra fascination for the thoughtful traveller
between the two. If you have been to Spain and dismissed
Portugal as 'another province' you will be delighted to learn
how wrong you have been.

So, go slowly through Portugal and give yourself time. With this
book in your hands you can avoid the tourist traps and strike
out to see how, and where, Portugal really ticks; for the people
who inhabit these pages are ready to become your friends.

Alastair Sawday

INTRODUCTION

How do we choose our Special Places?

Well, first of all we look for 'personality' — in the buildings and in their owners. As with people, so with houses. Then we consider the place, the architecture, contents, history, views and atmosphere. The beautiful is that which reveals its true nature; ugliness stems from falsity. So a small modern *pensão* can be as special in its way as a hotel, castle or monastery. Whatever the place, it will be run by good people, whether by a family who will welcome you to the dinner table as an old friend (the Portuguese are very hospitable) or staff who are discreet and helpful in a place where you are smitten by the architecture, exquisite furniture and antiques.

There has probably never been a better time to stay in Portugal, particularly since the advent of *turismo de habitação* and *turismo rural*, which have encouraged owners of historic and rural homes to open their doors to guests. Portugal is not a large country, but it has a wonderfully long history and great variations in landscape and character, and the old houses particularly are among the finest in the world: it is surprising how often, for example, we have discovered houses where the same family has lived for several centuries; a treat to enjoy a small slice of that tradition. Then there are the modern homes, full of light and space, and now the growing number of places which combine holidays with alternative spiritual and physical practices. This is a growing trend of such holidays in Portugal, a country whose own seductions are a rich culture, a benign climate and very good food.

There is the other side of Portugal, too, of course: the uncontrolled development of incongruous buildings, domestic and touristic. You can hardly travel anywhere in the world without seeing examples of that, but we consciously eschew the ugly, the dreary and the mass-produced look of chain hotels. We also ignore unfriendly hotels, noisy ones, or those which are over-priced.

What to expect

In most cases you will be staying in someone's home — with people who have families, jobs, sometimes pets, and friends. We choose them because we know they'll look after you. The Portuguese are convivial people who love the good things in life: company, conversation and good food and drink. Be prepared to be swept along by it all.

INTRODUCTION

Finding the right
place for you

It's our job to help you find a place you will like. We give honest
descriptions of our houses and owners and you should glean
from the write-up what the owners or housekeeper or staff
are like and how formal or casual the place is. The mention of
beautiful antiques should suggest that this may not be the place
to take your toddler, and phrases such as 'dress for dinner' tell
you that this isn't a place to slop around in shorts and T-shirt.
You should also be able to tell if it's the sort of house where you
can become a temporary member of the family, or somewhere
where you can have as much privacy as you like.

In each write-up there are clues about the mood of the house,
and there is an enormous variety within this book. The older
or larger ones may seem more immediately appealing, but don't
overlook the modern ones – they often have personality too.
In any place, it's always the people who create the atmosphere.

Map

How to use
this book

Look at the map at the front of the book, find your area, then
look for the places which are mapped. Note their numbers and
look up the same entry number which you will find at the
bottom of the page.

Rooms

We tell you the range of accommodation in single, double,
twin or triple rooms or in apartments, suites, cottages or
houses. Extra beds can often be added for children. Check
when booking.

Bathrooms

Those of you who like your bath should know that the length
of baths can vary from half to full length. In the south where
water is such a precious commodity you may prefer to shower.
And when you are packing do put in a bar of soap; the more
simple *hostal*-type places may not give you any and many of
the hotels will only have those tiny throw-away soaps which
are so difficult to find when you drop them in the bath.

In hotels, don't pull the cord which dangles above your bath
unless you are in dire straits. It is an alarm and may bring your
friendly receptionist rushing to your side.

INTRODUCTION

Prices

Prices are given for the room unless otherwise specified;
prices for singles can refer to single occupancy of a double
room. Breakfast is generally included in the price. Self-catering
prices are per apartment per day unless otherwise stated. Prices
for meals are per person.

The prices we quote were applicable at the time that this book
went to press. We publish every two years so expect prices to
be higher if you are using this book in 2004 or early 2005.

Symbols

There is an explanation of these on the last page of the book.
Use them as a guide, not as a statement of fact. If an owner has
a 'pets welcome' symbol, check in advance that your pet will
be welcome. Some told us that they only accept 'small' pets,
so will that include your Irish wolfhound puppies? Find out.
Equally, if an owner does not have the symbol that you're
looking for, it's worth discussing your needs; the Portuguese
generally love to please.

Quick Reference Indices

At the back of the book is a quick reference section to help
direct you to the places that suit you, be they self-catering,
suitable for wheelchair users, with pools or good walks close by.

Phones & Phone Codes

From Portugal to another country: dial 00 then add the
country code and then the area code without the first 0
e.g. ASP in Bristol, from Portugal: 01275 464891 becomes
00 44 1275 464891.

Within Portugal: simply dial the numbers given minus the
country code 351.
Calling Portugal from another country:
From the USA: 011 351 then the number.
From the UK: 00 351 then the number.

Land line numbers begin with 2, mobile phone numbers with 9
(and are more expensive).

The Portuguese phone system works well. As well as public
phone boxes (for which you can buy phonecards in most
newsagents) and phone boxes inside post offices (look for *Correios*),
virtually every café has a phone for which customers pay the
impulsos used, counted on a meter. (Café phones cost more.)

INTRODUCTION

Types of Properties

These pages reveal a plethora of different terms to describe the various hostelries. We include no star ratings in our guides; we feel they are limiting and misleading. This list serves as a rough guide to what you might expect to find behind each name.

Albergaria	An upmarket inn.
Casa	A house, old or new.
Castelo	A castle.
Estalagem	An inn, more expensive than an *albergaria*.
Herdade	A large farm or estate.
Monte	A long, low Alentejo farmhouse, usually built on top of a hill (*monte*).
Paço	A palace or country house.
Palacio	A palace or country house, but grander than a *paço*.
Pensão	A guesthouse; the Portuguese equivalent of a bed and breakfast, though breakfast is not always included in the price.
Quinta	A country estate or villa; in the Douro wine-growing area it often refers to a wine lodge's property.
Residencial	A guesthouse; usually slightly more expensive than a *pensao* and normally serving breakfast.
Solar	A manor house.

Practical Matters   Meals

We tell you if the owners offer lunches and dinners, and we give an average price (note that these are per person). It's often more relaxing to eat in say, after a long journey, than go out, and it is often necessary to book in advance, but Portugal has so many restaurants and cafés that whether you're in town, village or country, there will be a place offering freshly-cooked food nearby.

It is surprisingly inexpensive to eat out in Portugal. The set meal – *ementa turistica* – may offer a small choice, while à la carte – *á lista* – is a full choice. The dish of the day – *prato do día* – is usually a local speciality and helpings can be enormous. It is perfectly normal to ask for a *meia dose* – half portion – or for two adults to ask for *uma dose* – a portion – to share between two.

INTRODUCTION

When you sit down at virtually any restaurant in Portugal you will be given things to nibble before your meal arrives – olives, *chouriço* (spicy sausage), sardine spread. But, do remember – you will be charged for whatever you eat.

Bacalhao – salt cod – is the national dish: there are said to be 365 different ways of preparing it! Pork (as in Spain) is also much used. And don't despise the humble sardine – it is often the cheapest item on the menu and can be very good. (See the back of the book for more information on food). The basic mix for the ubiquitous *salada mista* is lettuce, tomato, onions. You can ask for it *sem azeite* – without olive oil. Grilled fish is often served scattered with fresh garlic; you could ask for it without: *sem alho*. Puddings are normally very sweet.

Seasons and Public Holidays

In Portugal everything closes down at Easter, Christmas and New Year, and on the following public holidays:

April 25	Commemorating the 1974 Revolution
May 1	Labour Day
early June	Corpus Christi
June 10	*Dia de camões e das Comunidades* – Camões Day
August 15	The Feast of the Assumption
October 5	Republic Day
November 1	All Saints Day
December 1	Immaculate Conception

There are also festivals for the saints and other commemorations. The Portuguese love festivals and there are lots during the summer. If there's one on near you, don't miss it. Here are some of the major festivals:

May Queima das Fitas celebrates the end of the academic year in Coimbra.

Fátima Portugal's most famous pilgrimage; also in October.

June Feira Nacional at Santarém lasts for 10 days, starting on the first Friday.

Festa de São Gonçalo in Amarente; first weekend.

Santos Popularos in Lisbon – celebrations in honour of St Anthony (13th), St John (24th) and St Peter (29th). There is also a festival in Porto for St John on the same date.

INTRODUCTION

July *Festa do Colete Encarnado* in Vila Franca de Xira with Pamplona-style running of bulls through the streets; first two weeks.

August *Romaria da Nossa Senhora da Agonía* in Viana do Castelo; third weekend.

September *Romaria da Nossa Senhora dos Remédios* in Lamego. Pilgrimage.

6th-8th 'New Fair' in Ponte de Lima; second and third weekend.

October *Feira de Outubro* in Vila Franca de Xira – more bull running.

Fátima second great pilgrimage of the year.

November *Feira Nacional do Cavalo* National Horse Fair in Golegã.

Booking

Try to book well ahead if you plan to be in Portugal during the holidays. August is very busy in the tourist and beach areas so you might choose to head for the more remote places in this book. Many hotels will ask you for a credit card number when you make your reservation. And remember to let smaller places know if you want dinner.

There's a bilingual booking form at the back of the book. Hotels often send back a signed or stamped copy as confirmation. Note: hotels don't necessarily assume that you are expecting a speedy reply!

Cancellations

Please give as much notice as possible and check cancellation terms and conditions when booking.

Registration

Many city hotels will only hold a reservation until the early evening, even though you might have booked months in advance. So ring ahead to let them know if you are planning to arrive late. (It remains law that you register on arrival in a hotel. Hotels have no right, once you have done so, to keep your passport.)

INTRODUCTION

Payment

Cash is always an acceptable method of payment but many places in this book also accept payment by credit card and have that symbol. The most commonly accepted credit cards are Visa, MasterCard and Eurocard. Many smaller places don't take plastic because of high bank charges; these will be marked with the 'piggy bank' symbol. There is nearly always a cash dispenser (ATM) close at hand; again Visa, MasterCard and Eurocard are the most useful.

Euros

We include a conversion chart at the end of this book.

Plugs

Virtually all sockets now have 220/240 AC voltage (usually 2-pin). Pack an adaptor if you travel with electrical appliances.

Driving & Car Hire

Driving in Portugal, especially the north, requires patience. The maps at the front of this book are to give you an approximate idea of where places are but do take a detailed road map with you. The worst time to drive is on any of the public holidays listed earlier when there is a massive exodus towards the countryside and the coast.

It is compulsory to have in the car: a spare set of bulbs, a warning triangle, a fire extinguisher and a basic first aid kit.

Don't forget your driving licence: if you are hiring a car you will need it and it is an offence to drive without it.

And remember that foreign number plates attract attention in the big cities so never leave your car with valuables inside. Use a public car park; they are cheap and safe.

Public Transport

You meet more people, and get much more of a feel for the country by travelling this way. Portugal is not a large country and you can get almost everywhere easily and efficiently by train or bus. Trains are often cheaper and some lines are very scenic, but it's almost always quicker to go by bus — especially on shorter journeys. If you are planning a quick trip by bus avoid buses marked *carreiras* (or CR). *Carreiras* might mean 'in a hurry' but these are the slowest of slow local buses and stop everywhere.

INTRODUCTION

Security

A degree of caution is necessary in the larger cities especially in the narrow side streets. Best not to carry ostentatious bags or cameras.

Children

The Portuguese love children, and most houses have the 'Children Welcome' symbol; indeed, most owners were surprised that we even asked the question. The absence of it means different things in different houses; some houses will welcome babies but don't relish the thought of youngsters tearing along corridors lined with antiques and figurines, so do enquire if the place appeals. We found that most owners have a flexible attitude.

Pets

Some people can't bear to leave home without transporting a beast of some sort with them, and the 'Pets Welcome' symbol means you can probably take your animal into the home; the criteria vary, often according to size and level of training (see Symbols above). Livestock may be allowed in bedrooms or housed outside. Do check in advance.

Smoking

Many Portuguese like to smoke, and it's particularly noticeable in restaurants and cafés. Most houses have no restrictions, but a growing number are introducing some sort of segregation and offering smoke-free rooms.

Tipping

Tipping is not as widespread as in the UK and US. However, the more expensive restaurants do expect a 10% service charge, if it is not already included.

Portuguese Tourist Offices

UK 2nd floor, 22/25 Sackville Street, London W1X 1DE (tel: 0207 494 1441)

USA 590 Fifth Avenue, New York 10036-4704 (tel: 212 354 4403) e-mail: tourism@portugal.org

INTRODUCTION

Environment

We try to be as 'green' as possible. We lend bicycles to staff and provide a pool car. We celebrate the use of organic, home-grown and locally produced food. We are working to establish an organic standard for B&Bs and run an Environmental Business Trust to stimulate business interest in the environment.

We also publish *The Little Earth Book*, a collection of essays on environmental issues. A new title, *The Little Food Book*, is another hard-hitting analysis – this time of the food industry. To try to reduce our impact on the environment we plant trees: the emissions directly related to our office, paper production, printing and distribution have been 'neutralised' through the planting of indigenous woodlands with Future Forests. We are, officially, Carbon Neutral.

Subscriptions

Owners pay to appear in this guide; their fee goes towards the inspection and production costs. We only include places and owners that we find positively special. It is not possible for anyone to buy their way in.

Internet

Our web site www.specialplacestostay.com has online pages for all the places featured here and in our other books. For more details see the back of the book.

Disclaimer

We make no claims to be objective in choosing our *Special Places To Stay*. They are here because we like them. Our opinions and tastes are ours alone and this book is a statement of them; we hope that you share them.

We have done our utmost to get our facts right but apologise unreservedly for any mistakes that may have crept in. Sometimes, too, prices shift, usually upwards, and 'things' change. Please tell us about any errors or changes.

And finally

Thank you to all those who have taken the time to share your opinions with us. You have helped make this edition of the book even better than the last!

Please let us have your comments; there is a report form at the back of this book. Or e-mail us at portugal@sawdays.co.uk

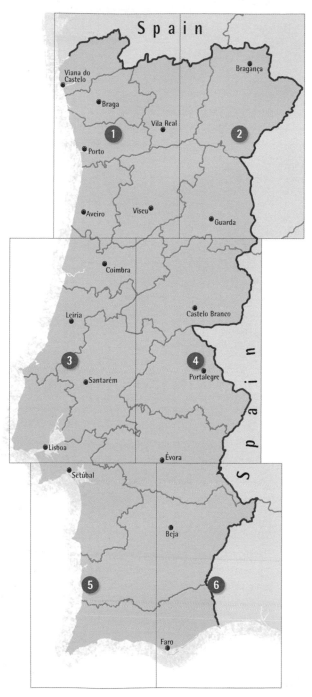

A guide to our map page numbers

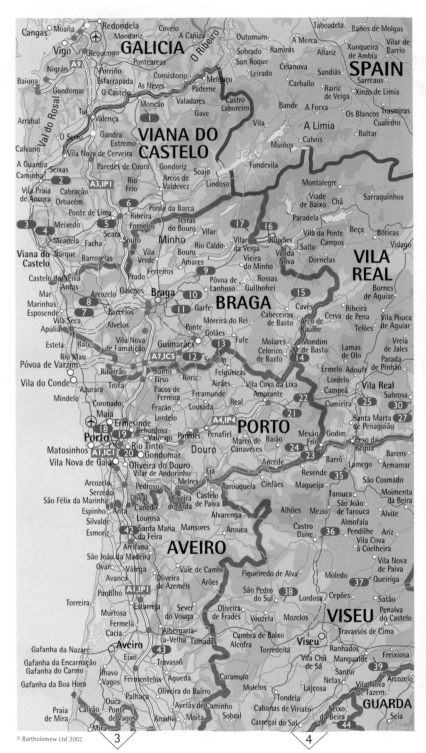

Map 1

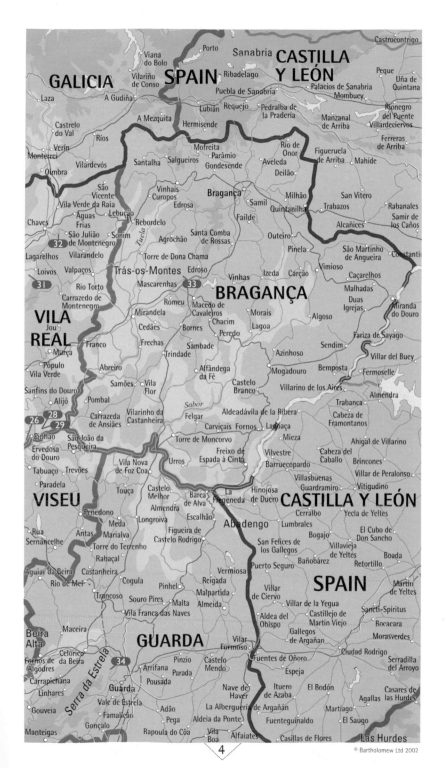

GALICIA

SPAIN

CASTILLA Y LEÓN

Castrocontrigo

Viana do Bolo
Porto
Sanabria
Peque
Uña de Quintana

Vilariño de Conso
Ribadelago
Palacios de Sanabria
Mombuey

Laza
A Gudiña
Puebla de Sanabria
Rionegro del Puente

Castrelo do Val
Ríos
Lubián
Requejo
Pedralba de la Pradería
Manzanal de Arriba
Villardeciervos

Verín
A Mezquita
Hermisende
Ferreras de Arriba

Monterrei
Mofreita
Río de Onor
Figueruela de Arriba
Mahide

Olmbra
Vilardevós
Santalha
Salgueiros
Parâmio
Gondesende
Aveleda
Deilão

São Vicente
Vinhais Curopos
Bragança
Milhão
San Vitero

Vila Verde da Raia
Edrosa
Samil
Quintanilha
Trabazos
Rabanales

Chaves
Águas Frias
Lebução
Rebordelo
Failde
Alcañices
Samir de los Caños

São Julião de Montenegro
Sonim
Agróchão
Santa Comba de Rossas
Outeiro
São Martinho de Angueira
Constanti

Lagarelhos
Vilarandelo
Torre de Dona Chama
Pinela
Vimioso

Loivos
Valpaços
Trás-os-Montes
Edroso
Vinhas
Izeda
Carção
Caçarelhos

VILA REAL
Rio Torto
Mascarenhas
BRAGANÇA
Malhadas
Duas Igrejas
Miranda do Douro

Carrazedo de Montenegro
Rómeu
Macedo de Cavaleiros
Morais

Jou
Mirandela
Chacim
Lagoa
Algoso

Murça
Cedães
Bornes
Peredo
Fariza de Sayago

Póbulo Vila Verde
Franco
Frechas
Sâmbade
Sendim
Villar del Buey

Sanfins do Douro
Abreiro
Trindade
Azinhoso
Bemposta
Fermoselle

Alijó
Samões
Vila Flor
Alfândega da Fé
Mogadouro
Villarino de los Aires

Pombal
Sabor
Castelo Branco
Trabanca
Almendra

Carrazeda de Ansiães
Vilarinho da Castanheira
Felgar
Aldeadávila de la Ribera
Cabeza de Framontanos

Pinhão
São João da Pesqueira
Carviçais
Fornos
Lagoaça
Ahigal de Villarino

Ervedosa do Douro
Torre de Moncorvo
Mieza
Cabeza del Caballo
Brincones

Tabuaço
Trevões
Vila Nova de Foz Coa
Urros
Freixo de Espada à Cinta
Vilvestre
Villar de Peralonso

Paradela
Touça
Barca de Alva
Barruecopardo
Villasbuenas
Guardramiro
Vitigudino

VISEU
Castelo Melhor
La Fregeneda
Hinojosa de Duero
CASTILLA Y LEÓN

Penedono
Almendra
Escalhão
Abadengo
Cerralbo
Yecla de Yeltes

Rua
Meda
Longroiva
Lumbrales
El Cubo de Don Sancho

Sernancelhe
Antas
Marialva
Figueira de Castelo Rodrigo
San Felices de los Gallegos
Bogajo
Villavieja de Yeltes
Boada

Torre do Terrenho
Rabaçal
Puerto Seguro
Bañobárez
Retortillo

Aguiar da Beira
Castanheira
Vermiosa
SPAIN

Rio de Mel
Cogula
Reigada
Villar de Ciervo
Martín de Yeltes

Trancoso
Pinhel
Malpartida
Almeida
Villar de la Yegua
Sancti-Spíritus

Souro Pires
Malta
Aldea del Obispo
Castillejo de Martín Viejo
Bocacara

Maceira
Vila Franca das Naves
Vilar Formoso
Gallegos de Argañán
Morasverdes

Beira Alta
GUARDA
Fuentes de Oñoro
Ciudad Rodrigo
Serradilla del Arroyo

Celorico da Beira
Pinzio
Castelo Mendo
Espeja

Fornos de Algodres
Serra da Estrela
Arrifana
Parada
Nave de Haver
Ituero de Azaba
El Bodón
Casares de las Hurdes

Carrapichana
Pousada
La Alberguería de Argañán
Martiago
Agallas

Linhares
Guarda
Adão
Pega
Aldeia da Ponte
Fuenteguinaldo
El Saugo

Gouveia
Vale de Estrela
Famalição
Gonçalo

Manteigas
Rapoula do Côa
Vila Boa
Alfaiates
Casillas de Flores
Las Hurdes

4

© Bartholomew Ltd 2002

Map 2

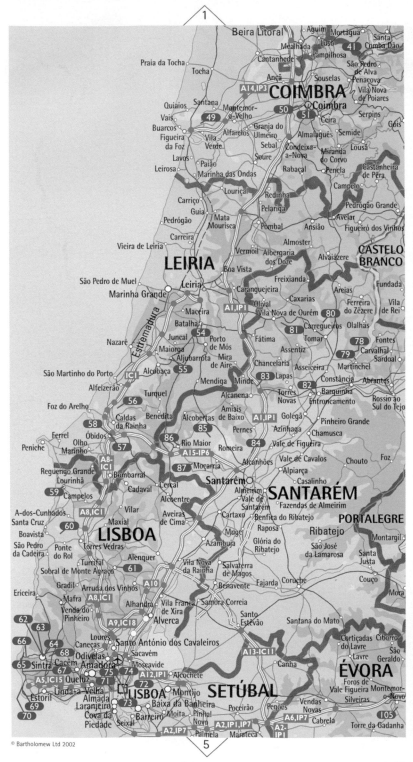

Map 3

© Bartholomew Ltd 2002

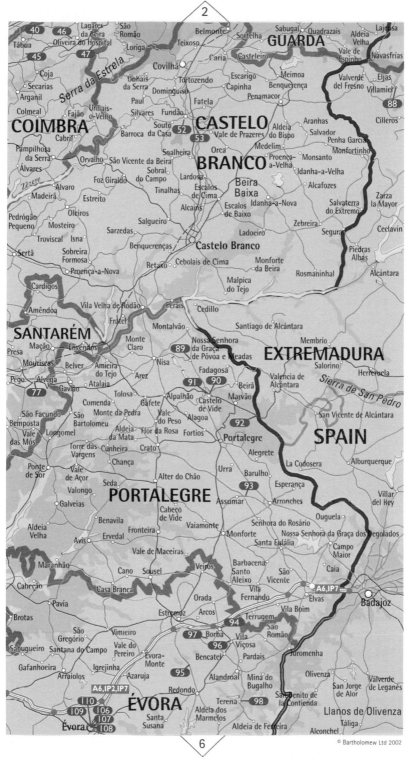

© Bartholomew Ltd 2002

Map 4

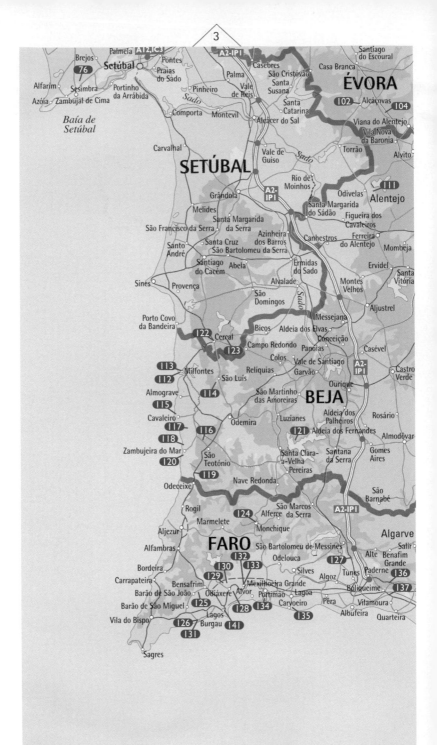

Map 5

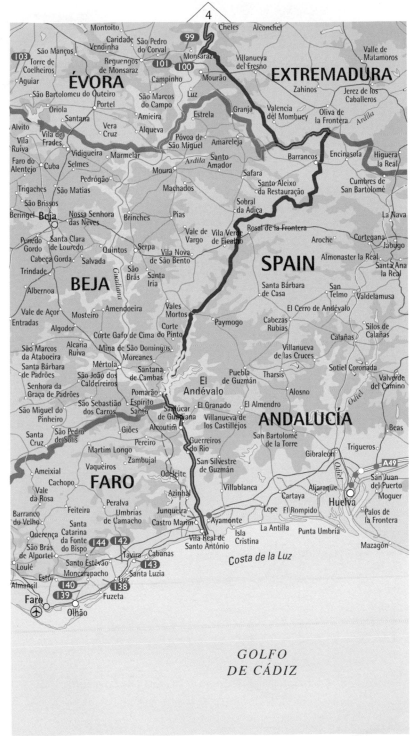

Map 6

NORTHERN PORTUGAL

"To enter Portugal from Spain is to come form a baked, dusty, tattered, plain into a well-kept garden."

HANS CHRISTIAN ANDERSEN

Casa de Rodas
4950 Monção, Viana do Castelo

Casa de Rodas is certainly a sight for (city) sore eyes; a long sweep of lawn bordering the main drive, then in the distance the low, clean-cut manor house with its chapel grafted onto one flank. This impressive home has been in the family for more than 400 years but don't expect your hosts to be pretentious about their aristocratic lineage: Maria Luisa's casual manner and her genuine friendliness when she greets you are a lovely appetiser for the experience of being here. There are a number of reception rooms on the ground floor, each quite different from the next; they have marvellous wooden ceilings, stucco and panelling, *trompe l'oeil* marble and painted friezes. The overall effect is festive and fun. There are family antiques, portraits and photos; masses of books and comfy sofas to read them in, a grandfather clock, piano and games table. The bedrooms are just as memorable. Each one is different, most vast, each with its own dressing room. The newer rooms are beautiful too and have bigger bathrooms and their own balconies but less of a feel for the past. Our inspector purred, "one of the most beautiful houses I've visited… a knockout place".

rooms	10 doubles/twins.
price	€ 75; single € 65.
meals	None available.
closed	Rarely.
directions	From Valença, just after turn to Monção, right at 'Turismo de Habitaçâo' sign. Gateway to house after 200m.

Maria Luisa Távora
tel   +351 251 652105

map 1   entry 1

Casa de Esteiró

Vilarelho, 4910-605 Caminha, Viana do Castelo

A magical old house that reflects the warm, outgoing personalities of owners José and Maria, the Casa de Esteiró is a rich experience from the moment you pass under the rugged stone archway. This late-18th-century house is extremely handsome and decorated with antiques and fine furniture – traditional Portuguese as well as finds from the owners' years abroad in the diplomatic service. The gallery is long, with masses of comfortable seating, beautiful cushions, porcelain and paintings, plus a lovely granite fireplace. The library is exquisite, and there is a small chapel off it (ask about the altar carried by the great-grandfather during the Peninsular War). The bedrooms too have both Portuguese and foreign furnishings, and are fresh with garden flowers. The self-catering apartments have their own living rooms, but guests are also welcome in the main house. Breakfast is served either in the bedrooms or in the huge dining room, lined with beautiful ceramic dishes. Outside: a good pool and a garden with many specimen trees (planted by an earlier owner, Viscount Negrelos), which thrive in this Minho climate... and some delightful quiet areas for sitting and listening to the running water and birds.

rooms	9: 7 doubles, 2 singles. Self-catering apartments.
price	€ 70; single € 55; apartment for 2, € 70; apartment for 4, € 120.
meals	Available locally.
closed	Rarely.
directions	Follow Viana do Castelo road to Valença on N13. Arrive in Caminha, right at sign for Centre & 'Turismo de Habitação'. After 50m, right at sign Casa de Esteiró.

José Manuel Villas-Boas

tel	+351 258 721333
fax	+351 258 921356
web	www.ciberguia.pt/casa-esteiro

Casa Santa Filomena

Estrada de Cabanas, Afife, 4900-012 Viana do Castelo

A grand entrance gate beckons you in to the Casa Santa Filomena, a solid, stonewalled building that was built in the 1920s. It is hidden away in a quiet corner of an already quiet village; your rest is assured. When we visited in early spring the old wisteria was a riot of tumbling lilac and mauve, as pretty a welcome as you could wish for. A high wall runs round the property; it girdles a small vineyard where *vinho verde* grapes are grown. Elsewhere the profusion of flowers is heady proof of the micro-climate that this part of the Minho enjoys; it seems as if anything will grow here, and your breakfast juice will come from the oranges in the garden. The rooms are rather functional but perfectly clean and comfortable. Your hosts and their staff are extremely helpful, and José himself has a passion for collecting and restoring carriages. When he is around, do ask to see them: they are a delight. This is a charming and secluded spot, and very good value. Among other diversions, a swimming pool and tennis courts are just a kilometre away, wonderful beaches not much further.

rooms	4 doubles/twins, 1 suite.
price	€45-€50; suite €55.
meals	Available locally.
closed	Rarely.
directions	From Valença to Viana, 1st left to Afife. From Viana 1st right. In centre of Afife turn inland (Estrada de Cabanas). House on left at first junction.

José Street Kendall

tel	+351 258 981619
fax	+351 226 175936
e-mail	soc.com.smiths@mail.telepac.pt

map 1   entry 3

Casa do Ameal

Rua do Ameal 119, Meadela, 4900-585 Viana do Castelo

Casa do Ameal has now been absorbed into the urban fabric of Viana, but the moment you pass into the entrance courtyard with its box hedges and gurgling fountain the outside world is left far behind. The estate was bought in 1669 by the de Faria Araújo family whose numerous descendants still watch over the place; there are 14 siblings in the present generation, five of the sisters still live at the house and most of the others arrive at the weekend! These loveable elderly ladies welcome you with tea and a tour of the house; they will proudly show off the collection of handicrafts and the family costume 'museum' which includes such delights as their grandparents' christening robes. Accommodation is in two guest rooms and seven apartments, some sleeping two, others four; most have their own kitchenette. The rooms are furnished in a simple, rustic style that goes well with the exposed stone walls. The sisters speak English, French and Spanish and will gladly help you plan your excursions to Viana do Castelo, where there are good restaurants, just two kilometres away.

rooms	2 doubles; 7 apartments.
price	€70; single €63. Apartments for 2, €75, for 4, €120.
meals	For larger groups, by request.
closed	Rarely.
directions	From Porto, N13/IC1 for Viana do Castelo. In Meadela, pass main square & church to supermarket 'Continente'. Left, pass car park, up hill. House on left.

Maria Elisa de Magalhães Faria Araújo
tel +351 258 822403

Casa de Pomarchão

Arcozelo, 4990-068 Ponte de Lima, Viana do Castelo

Casa de Pomarchão dates all the way back to the 15th century but owes its present look to a rebuild of 1775 when a baroque chapel and veranda were added. The manor is at the centre of a 60-hectare estate of vineyards and thick pine forest. Your choice is between an apartment in the wonderful main building (every inch the aristocrat's residence) or your own solidly built house. Some are classical in style (Milho and Bica), others have a more rustic feel (Toca and Mato). What is so delightful is their utter comfort; no corners have been cut. The houses all have hearths, top-quality sofas, warm curtains, paintings, good beds and well-equipped kitchens. French windows take you out to your own garden or terrace and the whole of the estate is yours for walking. You can swim in the huge old water tank, visit nearby Ponte de Lima and the beach is just a short drive away. This is a wonderful place to head for if you are planning a longer stay in Portugal. Frederico's wife greets you with a smile; she speaks excellent English. And you'll be loathe to pack your suitcase and to say goodbye to (we quote our inspector) "the biggest, softest dog I have ever seen".

rooms	8 self-catering apartments & houses.
price	For 2 €65–€70; for 4 €115–€130.
meals	Restaurants nearby.
closed	10-30 December.
directions	2km outside Ponte de Lima on N201 to Valença. Signed.

Frederico Villar

tel	+351 258 741742
fax	+351 258 742742
e-mail	informacors@casadepomarchao.com

map 1   entry 5

Casa da Várzea

Várzea, Beiral do Lima, 4990-545 Ponte de Lima, Viana do Castelo

You'll see Casa da Várzea as you wind your way up from the valley below. It would be hard not to fall in love with the beauty of the place, cradled among terraced vineyards. It lay abandoned for many years, but Inácio Caldas da Costa, whose feelings ran deep for the house where he was born, took courage and after his retirement set about the restoration of the family seat. Várzea has six big, light and charmingly decorated rooms. Family antiques are here for you to enjoy; you may find yourself in grandmother's or great-uncle's bed, made in cherry. Bedrooms are large and cool, and one has a lovely old Minho chest with a secret drawer for hiding gold sovereigns. Prints and framed embroidery, polished wooden floors and rugs are endearingly domestic. And in the public rooms wood-clad floors and ceilings lend warmth to grandeur. At breakfast there are long views from the airy dining room, plus home-made jams and fruit from the farm; dinner will probably be fish. There's a library, a pool-with-a-view and the old wooden 'drying house', now a second lounge/playroom – and a bar for tasting local *vinho verde*. Above all, Inácio and his wife will give you a genuinely warm welcome.

rooms	6 doubles/twins; 1 apartment for 4.
price	€ 75; single € 63. Apartment for 2 € 75, for 4 € 100.
meals	Dinner € 12, on request.
closed	Rarely.
directions	Leave Porto-Valença m'way at Viana do Castelo, P. Lima, P. Barca, following signs for Ponte da Barca for 6km to S. Martinho Gandra. Right to Beiral for 2km, church on left; entrance on left after 200m.

Inácio Barreto Caldas da Costa

tel	+351 258 948603
fax	+351 258 948412
e-mail	casadavarzea@iol.pt

Quinta do Convento da Franqueira
Carvalhal CC 301, 4755-104 Barcelos, Braga

This wonderful 16th-century monastery is hidden away among pine trees, cork oaks, eucalyptus and cypress. It is rich in history, and the cloister is thought to have been built with stones from the ruins of the castle of Faria. Certainly the brothers came here for the splendid isolation and the spring which now feeds a swimming pool, built above ornamental steps and with excellent views of house and church. Five centuries on, the granite buildings have been restored to their former grace by the Gallie family, a labour of love for 'how things were'; the results are delightful. Rooms and suite are lovely, generously proportioned and with fine antiques. There's a four-poster in one room, old prints, pretty bedside lamps and tables and stuccoed ceilings. All are individual and even the bathrooms have hand-painted tiles. The estate produces its own *vinho verde* from vineyards that roll right up to Franqueira's walls; Piers Gallie enjoys showing guests round the winery. Children have swings in the gardens and a rocking horse in the play room. A huge tiled terrace overlooks lush gardens. Try to visit the Thursday market in nearby Barcelos.

rooms	5: 4 doubles/twins, 1 suite.
price	€ 100.
meals	Available locally.
closed	November–May.
directions	From Braga, N103 to Barcelos; at end of N103 right round ring road. Pass Renault garage, then 2nd right for Póvoa de Varzim. Under bridge, then left to Franqueira. Through village; middle road of three up hill into woods to bar. Right, then left after church.

Piers & Kate Gallie

tel	+351 253 831606
fax	+351 253 832231

map 1   entry 7

Quinta do Tarrio

Tamel, Santa Leocádia, 4750 Barcelos, Braga

A farm with 300 years of history, this delightful place sits in gardens of lawns, flowers, orange, lemon, pear and plum trees and is surrounded by vineyards and a kiwi plantation. Owners Marine, who is Swedish, and George, who spent much of his early life in Norway, are informal and welcoming. They will show you the farm's *adega* where the famous local *vinho verde* is produced – worth visiting for a tasting. The farmhouse is full of interesting antiques and ancient farming artefacts and has lots of space; guests can relax in the *sala*, a room of tile floors and rugs, with splendid views over the garden, orchards and beyond. In colder weather there are open log fires and woodburning stoves are lit. Bedrooms are comfortable and quiet with pretty curtains and cushions and their beds are large, with twin beds zipped together to make doubles. Everything here is on a grand scale, not least the breakfasts; the juice comes from the estate-grown oranges and the home-made jams include kiwi. The grounds are full of variety, there's an attractive pool area, tennis court and space to play handball, volleyball and basketball. *Minumum stay three days.*

rooms	5: 4 doubles/twins, 1 suite.
price	€80; suite for 2, €80, suite for 4, €110.
meals	Available locally.
closed	November–April.
directions	From IC1 exit for Barcelos-Braga, then follow N205 until N103, then turn twice towards Viana do Castelo, until a r'bout. On 50m & right to Tamel Sta. Leocádia. 1km to Quinta.

Marine & George Ennis
tel	+351 253 881558
fax	+351 253 882773

Quinta de São Vicente

Lugar de Portas, Geraz do Minho, 4830-315 Póvoa do Lanhoso, Braga

This is an address ideal for those who love the grape, for the Minho's delightful *vinho verde* is produced here (the 'green', incidentally, refers to age not colour) and you can visit and buy from the *adega*. Teresa and her husband will share much more wine-talk should you stay with them at this old bougainvillaea-clad farmhouse. This is an enchanting place: relaxed, solidly comfortable, not a bit ostentatious. An enormous drawing room feels more like a conservatory with high windows opening on two sides, with family photos, a woodburner and plenty of sofa space. The dining room is off to one end; at breakfast, expect a big spread and a chance to admire the large collection of porcelain. In warmer weather you will eat out under the orange trees with a view of the vineyards. And your sleep should be deep; bedrooms are manicured, large and light. Cor de Rosa has its own veranda, Amerelo would be perfect for a family, Azul is rather smaller but pretty just the same. Ask to be shown the unusual paintings in the Quinta's chapel (1623) and find time to visit the diminutive castle of nearby Póvoa do Lanhoso.

rooms	5 doubles/twins; 1 self-catering house.
price	€ 60. House for 2, € 80; for 4, € 120.
meals	Dinner € 15, with wine, by arrangement.
closed	Rarely.
directions	From Porto A3 north, exit onto N103 for Braga/Chaves. Turn off for Amares then, after 1.5km, left for Geraz, Ferreiros & Covelas. Signed.

Teresa V Ferreira

tel	+351 253 632466
fax	+351 253 632466
e-mail	quintadesaovicente@yahoo.com

map 1   entry 9

Castelo de Bom Jesus

Bom Jesus, 4710-455 Braga

The Castelo de Bom Jesus looks down over the city of Braga and all the way to the Atlantic coast. Enter beneath the grand portal sculpted with the family coat of arms: the blue-blooded Meirelles have lived here since the 18th century. The outside was remodelled in the neo-Gothic style and has been alikened to a fairy-tale castle; the present generation of the family restored the interiors. Some rooms are as sumptuous as you'd expect, other less so; the presidential suite is the grandest, with *trompe l'oeil* frescoes, period furniture and jacuzzi. Suites have air-conditioning. Continental breakfast is served at a huge dining table in a graceful room beneath family portraits. When dinner is available it's a grand affair, in the oval, chandeliered dining room with its beautiful wrap-around fresco of arches and gardens. In the long lounge are grand piano and harp; a second salon is given over to the billiard table. You are near a busy road, but the gardens provide a buffer of green and calm where peacocks roam. Although this is generally considered an exotic port of call, some readers have felt that a slight air of neglect is creeping in: please let us know.

rooms	11: 9 doubles/twins, 2 suites.
price	€75; suite €125.
meals	Lunch/dinner €30.
closed	Rarely.
directions	From Porto A3, then N14 to Braga. Here follow signs for Bom Jesus to top of hill; right through gate just before Sanctuary car park.

Dr Manuel de Castro Meirelles

tel	+351 253 676566
fax	+351 253 677691
e-mail	res@armilarworldhotels.com
web	www.armilarworldusa.com

Casa dos Lagos
Bom Jesus, 4710-455 Braga

A warm, dignified welcome awaits you at Casa dos Lagos. The house was built by a viscount at the end of the 18th century on a wooded hillside which it shares with the Bom Jesus sanctuary; don't miss the extraordinary baroque staircase which zigzags up to the chapel on top of the hill, but do visit on a weekday to avoid the crowds of pilgrims. Both the devout and not so devout are welcome at Andrelina's home which is a lesson in quiet elegance. Light floods in through the French windows of the sitting/dining room; at one end there is a drop-leaf table beneath a fine chandelier (where there will be cake for breakfast), at the other is a velvet sofa drawn up to a large fireplace where you may sip a pre-dinner glass of port served from a cut-glass decanter. The terrace gives onto a garden where stands of camellia break up the order of carefully clipped box hedges and ornamental fountains; the views from here are breathtaking. Only one bedroom is in the main house. It is large, elegantly corniced and has a fine antique bedroom set: marble-topped dresser, cavernous wardrobe and ornately carved bed. Other rooms and the apartments are more modern and these, too, are large and well-equipped.

rooms	3 doubles/twins; 4 apartments.
price	€ 75; single € 63; apartment for 2, € 75, for 4, € 120.
meals	Available locally.
closed	Rarely.
directions	From Braga, EN103 to Bom Jesus. Here, right at signs.

Andrelina Pinto Barbosa

tel	+351 253 676738
fax	+351 253 679207
e-mail	casadoslagosbomjesus@oninet.pt

map 1   entry 11

Casa de Sezim

Apartado 2210, 4810 Guimarães, Braga

The owners must be fond of Casa de Sezim – it has been in the family for more than 700 years. The first grapes were trod here in 1390! Today the estate's *vinho verde* is of prize-winning quality. The elegant portal in Sezim's rich ochre façade (the present building is mostly 18th century) strikes a properly welcoming note and this grand old house – it bears the patina of long use – will seduce you with its understated elegance. You enter via an enormous, sober lounge with heavy old oak beams, granite floor and walls. The family coat of arms graces the hearth and blue-blooded forebears look down from their gilt frames – if only one could invite them down for a game of billiards. The fun really begins upstairs in the bedrooms. Some have four-poster beds, others have tapestried headboards, perhaps a writing desk; all have some antique pieces and rich patterns on wallpaper, bedspreads and curtains. But the gaily decorated panelling is their main joy. We'd probably sacrifice space and go for a tower room with a view. Also memorable are Sezim's panoramic paintings that date from the early 19th century with exotic scenes from the Old and the New Worlds.

rooms	10: 9 doubles/twins, 1 suite.
price	€60–€100; single €45–€78; suite €92.
meals	Lunch/dinner €23, by arrangement.
closed	Rarely.
directions	From Porto, A3 for Braga, then A7 to Guimarães. Then N105 for Santo Tirso. Right in Covas (after petrol station & Ford garage); house 2.2km further directly opposite. 'Tecidos ASA'.

António Pinto de Mesquita

tel	+351 253 523000
fax	+351 253 523196
e-mail	geral@sezim.pt
web	www.sezim.pt

Quinta de Cima de Eiriz

Lugar de Cima de Eiriz, Calvos, 4810-605 Guimarães, Braga

On a south-facing slope of the beautiful Penha mountain, this old Minho *quinta* has been completely restored. In the beamed and terracotta-tiled lounge, the old grape press has been transformed into an unusual raised bar. Marvel at the size of the granite lintels, flagstones and building blocks of the entrance hall. The pillar-box red of the doors and windows lends a lighter note. Bedrooms are in the old stable blocks, updated with central heating and phones and have sparkling marbled and tiled bathrooms. Most memorable are their views over the well-trimmed lawns and across the valley. Breakfast is a big meal; expect fresh orange juice, yogurts, several types of bread and cake and home-made jams. Afterwards you could walk straight out to explore the Penha National Park. In the warmer months you can plunge into the pool, while the balconied terrace is just right for a sundowner. There is also an excellent games room. The views are long and rural and only 10km away is Guimarães with its narrow streets, castle and superb municipal museum. Closer still is the Santa Marinha da Costa Monastery, the best preserved medieval building of the region.

rooms	4: 2 doubles, 2 twins.
price	€ 60.
meals	Available locally.
closed	Rarely.
directions	A3 Porto-Braga. In Vila Nova de Famalaicão, A7 to Guimarães. Then towards Fafe & Felgueiras. After 4km, right for Felgueiras for 4km, then right for Penha & Lapinha (ignore Penha & Calvos turn). After 2km, left at stone cross; signed.

Dr. João Gaspar de Sousa Gomes Alves

tel	+351 253 541750
fax	+351 253 420559

map 1   entry 13

Casa do Campo

Molares, 4890 Celorico de Basto, Braga

The Casa do Campo is every inch the classic *solar* or country manor. An enormous, ornately-sculpted portal and turreted outer wall protect the inner courtyard. The prize-winning formal gardens (which include an excellent swimming pool) are a hymn to the camellia – the country's oldest is said to be here and, thanks to careful topiary, they take on fabulous forms. The Meireles family has been here for centuries farming the estate and its vines. Maria Armanda receives her guests with natural grace. The bedrooms are in a renovated wing and are of the sort that we love; no two are the same, they are decorated in classical style and have polished wooden floors, elegantly stuccoed ceilings, cut flowers and a feeling of space. Breakfast in the classically elegant dining room with its beautiful paintings, cabinets of fine porcelain and carved ceiling; or there is a smaller, less formal dining room. Settle into the sitting room with its velvet chairs and old harpsichord or into the splendid old library. The manor's fine Renaissance chapel still has a weekly mass. *Room details change to four doubles and four suites in 2004.*

rooms	8: 7 doubles/twins, 1 suite.
price	€ 75; single € 62; suite approx. € 100.
meals	Lunch/dinner € 22, by arrangement.
closed	Christmas.
directions	From Braga, N101 to Guimarães, then N206 for Fafe, Celorico de Basto & Mondim. At Gandarela, right on N304 to Fermil; then right on N210 for Celorico. House signed after 1.5km.

Maria Armanda Meireles
tel	+351 255 361231
fax	+351 255 361231

Casa de Canêdo

Barreiro CP 101, 4890-140 Celorico de Basto, Braga

The setting for this 17th-century manor is superb: in a peaceful valley amid vineyards, forested hills and mountains. The new wing (early 19th century) is in granite, the older part rendered in earthy yellow. The centuries live side by side and bedrooms and suites are all different: the Romantic Room has a great mahogany double bed and looks over fields, the Cameleiras suite has a large sitting room and opens to a garden of camellias, the Quarto das Laranjeiras leads to an orange grove. The Chapel Room has Dona Maria twin beds and the Patio Room, which opens onto the inner courtyard and fountain, D. João V furniture. All have something special and the Senhora da Graça mountain is seen from several windows. The large lounge has plenty of sofas, a granite fireplace and an 18th-century oil of Our Lady; in the Piano Room is a 19th-century grand and old portraits. The dining room is wonderfully rustic, with long wooden table and fireplace, and walls and floor of granite. Outside are gardens and 90 acres of vineyards; the cellars are still used for the Casa's *vinho verde*. And most of the food here comes fresh from the farm.

rooms	9: 6 doubles/twins, 3 suites.
price	€ 75; single € 62; suite € 75-€ 100.
meals	Lunch/dinner € 17, by arrangement.
closed	15 December–15 January.
directions	On EN205 Cabaceiras de Basto-Amarante, between Arco de Baúlhe & Fermil de Basto, look for signs to house.

Maria José Silva
tel +351 255 361293
fax +351 255 361765

map 1   entry 15

Casa de Dentro 'Capitão-Mor'

Vila-Ruivães, C.180, 4850-341 Vieira do Minho, Braga

This was once the home of none other than Capitão-Mor de Ruivães who put the French to rout during the Peninsular War (the 'War of Independence' to the Portuguese). It sits proudly on one side of the valley which divides the Cabeira and Gerês mountain ranges in the tiniest of hamlets amid the terraced vineyards and deep greenery of the Minho. Both hosts and home exude warmth and welcome. Ilda, a retired school teacher, relishes sharing her intimate knowledge of this corner of the Minho: she has maps ready for your walks and will tell you about the region's fascinating mythology. We loved the sitting room with its low beams, granite hearth, old copper still and wall cabinets displaying the family china – just the place for settling down with a good book. The guest rooms are as unassuming as the rest of Ilda's home; they vary in size but all have antique beds and wardrobes, parquet floors, rugs and pretty bedside lamps. Breakfast is as generous as Ilda herself: yogurts, home-made jams, fruit juice and Ilda's very special cake, *bola de carne folar*. There is a tennis court, a pool-with-a-view and the wonderful Gerês Park right on your doorstep.

rooms	5 doubles/twins; 1 apartment for 6, with kitchenette.
price	€ 63; single € 50; apartment € 180–€ 190.
meals	Restaurants nearby.
closed	Rarely.
directions	From Braga, EN103 to Ruivães. House in centre of village, to right of church.

Ilda de Jesus Truta Fraga de Miranda Fernandes

tel	+351 253 658117
fax	+351 253 658117
e-mail	casadedentro@clix.pt

Casa Cabrilho

Lapela-Cabril, 5470-019 Lapela, Braga

Chef Antonio is determined to put this all-but-unknown mountain hamlet on the culinary map. He and his father make a good team: Antonio trained as a cook in Australia and London; Manuel, once a waiter on a cruise ship, tends the vegetable garden, most picturesquely sloped. So, you'll get more than rice and chips here: expect the freshest vegetables, the best local meats including *cabrito* (kid), the heartiest soups and stews. Bedrooms, in contrast, are an afterthought: small, with cork floors, nylon covers, bare ceiling bulbs, and the bathroom is shared (among members of the same party). Hardly a place for Sybarites, then, but valuable for those seeking an insight into the 'real' Portugal. Hearty hikers wanting to spend a night in these remote hills would be as happy as Larry. Mention must be made of the balustrade-free steps up the rooms and the sheer-drop terrace: leave adventurous offspring at home! Spend the day in the hills, return for a splendid supper, play a round of billiards, turn in for a quiet night. A no-frills place to stay simply miles from the beaten tourist track.

rooms	4 doubles.
price	€25; singles €20.
meals	Lunch/dinner €10.
closed	Rarely.
directions	From Braga, EN103 for 35km. Before Salamonde, turn off for Cabril for 21km to Lapela.

Antonio Goncalves
tel +351 253 659260
e-mail res.cabrilho@sapo.pt

map 1   entry 17

Pensão Estoril

Rua de Cedofeita 193, 4050-179 Porto

We include this little family-run boarding house because it is central, clean and a good base if your purse doesn't stretch to the rather grander hotels of Porto. Rua de Cedofeita is one of the city's liveliest (pedestrianised) shopping streets. Halfway along, Pensão Estoril occupies a 1900s townhouse. The pension – reached by the original bannistered staircase winding its elegant way up to the top floor – has been in the care of Benvinda and Joaquim for many years. Kinder folk you could not hope to meet. Bedrooms are simple, some of them curiously shaped around the bath and shower rooms which were added piecemeal over the years. We'd prefer one of those looking out over the garden at the back, a rare expanse of green in this part of the city. Most have small shower rooms, are carpeted and have phones, and the upstairs ones are surprisingly quiet. The terrace to the rear looks out across the garden, a place to unwind after a day of visits in this fascinating city. A reliable and inexpensive alternative with good food downstairs and plenty of places to eat close by.

rooms	16 doubles/twins/family, 1 quadruple.
price	€31–€41; single occ. €28–€34; family €44–€57; quad. €38–€48.
meals	Available locally.
closed	Rarely.
directions	Follow signs to Porto centre; head for 'Palácio de Cristal & Torre dos Clérigos', then 'Praça Coronel Pacheco' (ask). Park in 'Praça Coronel Pacheco' in front of police station. Estoril 100m.

Benvinda & Joaquim Santos

tel	+351 22 200 2751
fax	+351 22 208 2468
e-mail	jsantos98@softhome.net

Casa do Marechal

Avenida da Boavista 2674, 4100-119 Porto

Elegant, cream and white, utterly-Deco Casa do Marechal was built in 1940 and would sit as happily on the sea front in Miami as it does here in one of Porto's smarter residential areas. It looks like a wedding cake, with a rich layer of cream stucco running round at second-floor level. Things are just as flamboyant inside; the present owners have transformed an already grand house into a refined and luxurious guest house. There are just five bedrooms, in pink, blue, green, beige and yellow. They are a good size and carefully manicured; beds are five-star, and each room has a small writing table and all the usual modern extras, even hydro-massage tubs with sparkling tiles all round. There is an orange-coloured lounge with a balcony, a roof terrace and a garden with shady corners. At breakfast you can expect all the normal things plus fresh fruit and even porridge. The restaurant serves dinners most days; everything's bought fresh at the local market. The owners describe the food as "a new gastronomic interpretation of French and Portuguese traditional cuisine", and vegetarian food can be provided too. (You may need the gym, sauna and Turkish bath in the basement!).

rooms	5 doubles/twins.
price	€ 155; single € 145.
meals	Lunch/dinner € 30. Restaurant closed Sunday & Monday.
closed	August & Christmas.
directions	Arriving on m'way from Lisbon, after toll booths, for Arrabida, then Boavista, then Foz & Castelo do Queijo. Hotel on right after 3km; with own parking.

João Paulo Baganha

tel	+351 226 104702
fax	+351 226 103241
e-mail	casa.marechal@mail.telepac.pt

map 1   entry 19

Residencial Castelo Santa Catarina

Rua Santa Catarina 1347, 4000-457 Porto

This eye-catching building was built high up above Porto during the period which the Portuguese call the Gothic Revival. Even if the corner turrets and window arches don't remind you of Notre Dame, you can't fail to be intrigued by this tile-clad edifice – it stands like a folly, surrounded by swaying palms, in an otherwise conservative suburb of the city. The interior décor is as extravagant as the building's exterior. You are regaled by gilt and stucco, chandeliers and mirrors, cherubs and lozenges, Tiffany lamps and roses, repro beds and cavernous wardrobes. It is showy, over the top, faded in parts, garish in others and incredible fun. Your choice of carpet colour? Turquoise, lime green or, perhaps, navy paisley. There is the odd patch of peeling paint, the bathroom tiles are often out of step with the rooms but the whiff of the past is a part of the charm. The owner's affable son João is normally about in reception and with fluent English can answer all your questions about this whimsical building. Try to book the suite in the tower; it's worth the extra for the views. An enormously entertaining city hotel.

rooms	24: 21 doubles/twins, 3 suites.
price	€63; single €43; suite €75.
meals	Restaurants nearby.
closed	Rarely.
directions	At top of Rua Santa Catarina, just below Plaza Marques Pombal. Follow signs & ask directions.

João Brás

tel	+351 225 095599
fax	+351 225 506613
e-mail	castelosantacatarina@iol.pt

Casal de Aboadela

Aboadela, 4600-500 Amarante, Porto

You'll long remember arriving at Aboadela. Once you turn off the main road you twist and turn along the narrowest of lanes to this delightfully sleepy hamlet and its old Douro farmhouse. There is many a treat in the rambling gardens: an old granite maize store, a bubbling spring, gourds and pumpkins drying in the sun, old millstones recalling the building's origins. There are roses and oranges and vines and, in among them, secluded places for contemplation; it would be a perfect place to paint or read, such is the peace. The bedrooms are in the main house, simply attired in cottage style with family furniture and lacking nothing; just to one side in a converted outbuilding is the 'stone little house' (sic) which is self-contained – with a barbecue – and would be just perfect for a longer stay. The guest sitting/dining room is similarly unpretentious: granite-walled with a tiled floor and potted plants. Home-grown wine is available. A French window gives onto a small balcony and lets in the morning light and the view. There are lovely rambles straight out from the house and the São Gonçalo monastery in Amarante is just a short drive away.

rooms	4: 3 doubles/twins, 1 suite; 1 house for 2.
price	€42; suite €50; house €55.
meals	Picnics on request.
closed	Rarely.
directions	From Amarante, IP4 for Vila Real. 9km after Amarante, right to Aboadela; follow signs for 'Turismo Rural', then 'TR' to house.

José Silva Rebelo

tel	+351 255 441141
e-mail	srebelo@med.up.pt

map 1   entry 21

Casa da Levada

Travanca do Monte, Cx. 715, Bustelo, 4600 Amarante, Porto

The great crenellated tower is visible as you come down the winding cobbled track into this ancient hilltop village, perched amid mountain views. Levada is really a small castle in a settlement built of rough-hewn, moss-covered granite blocks where people and animals still live cheek-by-jowl. Rough wooden doors open to reveal a goat, a pair of oxen, an old woman embroidering: scenes from centuries past. The house is a mountain refuge, and hosts Maria and Luís are wonderfully welcoming. She is an English teacher, he a humorous man whose family have lived here for 300 years. You'll sleep in bedrooms with granite walls, wooden ceilings, beams and sisal matting. The Tower Room has a separate bathroom across the landing, with low beams and a terracotta floor; the unusual Poet's Room has a trapdoor down to the bathroom. The lounge is comfortable and the dining room barn-like, with a large oval table at which everyone has breakfast (cooked by Luís) or dinner together: food is traditional and the wine comes from Luís's mother's farm. Up the hill, you pass granite water mills; further up is a bleak hilltop with great boulders and dolmens. An amazing place.

rooms	4 doubles/twins.
price	€52–€65.
meals	Dinner €20.
closed	Rarely.
directions	From Amarante, N101 for Regua to Cavalinho. After 6km, right at sign for house.

Maria & Luis Vasconcelos do Lago Mota

tel	+351 255 433833
fax	+351 255 433833
e-mail	casalevada@clix.pt

Casa d'Além

Oliveira, Mesão Frio, 5040-204 Caldas de Moledo, Porto

The cheerful façade of Casa d'Além looks out across the terraced vineyards of the Douro valley and reflects the optimism of the early 1920s. It also suggests a rather diminutive residence; however, behind its frontage the house widens out and becomes large and airy, with far more than first impressions would suggest. The public rooms are the most refined: the Rennie Mackintosh print on easy chairs, sofas and drapes is perfectly balanced by the delicate wrought-iron work of the balconies. Piano, card table and shining parquet create an atmosphere of old Portugal. Next door is a panelled dining room and, still more remarkable, a long painted corridor, a 'marbled sunburst', which leads to your bedroom. A feast of period pieces, there are rugs and marble-topped dressers, generous old tubs and wash stands. There are heavenly views from the rooms O Quarto do Avó and O Quarto Azul. Paulo and his wife speak excellent English and their marvellous housekeeper Maria will take care of you. Outside are views, pure air and a pleasing pool area. Be sure not to miss dinner: perhaps a roast from their bread oven, home-made ice-cream and a chilled glass of the local wine.

rooms	4 doubles/twins/family.
price	€ 75; single € 60; family € 100.
meals	Lunch/dinner € 17.50.
closed	Rarely.
directions	From Régua, N108 to Porto. After 3km in Granjaõ, pass under railway bridge, then right to Oliveira. House signed.

Paulo José F S Dias Pinheiro

tel	+351 254 321991
fax	+351 254 321991
e-mail	casadalem@clix.pt
web	www.casadalem.pt

map 1   entry 23

Casa das Torres de Oliveira

Oliveira, Vila Real, 5040 Mesão Frio, Porto

Arriving in Oliveira, you won't miss this magnificent twin-towered building sitting proudly on a hillside to one side of the village. This is a classic manor house, grand but welcoming. The estate's vineyards surround the house, and the grapes are for port as well as white and red Sedinhas, named after the present owner's seventh-removed grandfather who built the house. Cross a cobbled patio with a fountain to reach the main entrance; from here there are long views out across the valley and down to the river Douro which serpentines into the far distance. To one side of a high entrance hall, Oliveira's lounge is generous with space and light; it has a rugged parquet floor and sashed-back curtains to let in the glorious setting. Cushioned sofas, old china, a piano and a Madonna and Child speak of *velho Portugal*. From the high-ceilinged dining room – housing bottles of port going back to 1888 – you look out at the *adega* where vats of the estate's wine are stored; a bottle will be yours at dinner. Your bedroom will have a beautiful bed and dresser, rugs and lamps and a shining wooden floor; the tower room is a great favourite and worth the price.

rooms	6: 5 doubles/twins, 1 suite.
price	€92–€100; single €73–€77.
meals	Lunch €10; dinner, with wine, €17.
closed	November–March.
directions	From Porto, IP4 to Amarante. Then N101 for Mesão Frio, then N108 for Régua. In Granjão, left to Oliveira (just before bridge & signs 'Qtas du Douro'). After 3km, 2nd left to Oliveira: house on right.

Isidora Reguela Benito Sousa Girão

tel	+351 254 336743
fax	+351 254 336195
e-mail	casatorresoliveira@iol.pt

Casa das Cardosas
Rua Central, Folhadela, 5000-103 Vila Real

What views! Although you are just a mile from Vila Real this grand Trás-os-Montes manor enjoys as bucolic a setting as you could hope to find; the hills roll out before you, sprinkled with white villages and farmsteads. The Cardosa family has been here for more than 250 years and once made wine; the gardens produce peaches, plums, cherries and raspberries; there's a lovely pool. Find time to let the warm-natured Maria Teresa tell you a little of the area's history. Her three bedrooms are quiet, elegantly decorated and have not a hint of hotel. There are rugs and shining parquet, and one bedroom has a wonderfully ornate Bilros four-poster. The green room has a chandelier and pretty fabrics, and the smallest room has direct access to the terrace and its views. The lounge and dining room have parquet floors and period tables and chairs, while fresh flowers and family mementos displayed in glass wall cabinets encourage a mood of unaffected intimacy. Breakfast at Cardosas is a generous meal with home-made jams, juices and eggs; at dinner you may be treated to roast beef or hake from the wood-fired oven. Make sure you have time to explore the Alvão Natural Park.

rooms	3 doubles/twins.
price	€60; single €55.
meals	Lunch/dinner by arrangement.
closed	Rarely.
directions	In Vila Real head to university. Left of main entrance, house signed.

Maria Teresa Cardosa Barata Lima

tel	+351 259 331487
fax	+351 259 331487

map 1   entry 25

Quinta de la Rosa
5085-215 Pinhão, Vila Real

If you like port, then stay as guests of the Bergqvists. The family has been in the trade for nearly 200 years and, as is usual in the industry, the estate matures its wines in-house and sells direct to customers. What better incentive to come? But first a hard choice is yours, between a B&B room or your very own Douro farmhouse. Three new bedrooms share a terrace high above the Douro, while those in the main house are lower and nearer to the river. All are special; some have brightly-painted Alentejo furniture, others are more antique, and one has its own little lounge and a view of Pinhão. Of the two houses, each with its own pool, we loved Lamelas, hidden away at the very top of the estate and approached through a forest. It is splendidly decorated and equipped with space enough for a large family or group. Amerela (see large photo), further down the hill, has similar standards of décor. If you're not into self-catering, enjoy breakfast in the light, sunny dining room with more of that view; housekeeper Filomena will look after you. But first priority must be a tour of the cellars and a port tasting (followed, perhaps, by a cruise on the river). In September, join in with the grape harvest.

rooms	6: 5 doubles/twins, 1 suite; 2 self-catering houses for 6-8.
price	€63; suite €80; single €55. House €500-€1,000 per week.
meals	Good restaurants within walking distance.
closed	Rarely.
directions	Signed from Pinhão.

Sophia Bergqvist
tel	+351 254 732254
fax	+351 254 732346
e-mail	sophia@quintadelarosa.com
web	www.quintadelarosa.com

Quinta do Conde

Gouvinhas, Sabrosa, 5060 Vila Real

This old stone house has character and quality. Housekeeper Lucia is kindness itself, very helpful, and proud of the house, which is spotlessly clean. The views over the hills and down the valley are stunning, and the house, set in a vineyard, has a lovely feel thanks to exposed stone walls, slate floors and chestnut shutters, doors, wardrobes and panelling – all so well-made. The bedrooms are individual, not overly fussy, and have comfortable beds and good views; three of the twin rooms have fairly modern bathrooms, and the quality throughout is good. The two sitting rooms are inviting – one has stone floors, rugs and sofas, the other slate floors, a sofa, card table and wood panel ceiling. The dining room is well proportioned and centres on a 10-seat round table with granite base. At the front of the house there are places to sit and enjoy the magnificent views of Trás-os-Montes, which you can also enjoy from the poolside. Ideal for those who want to get away from it all, not forgetting that the area has much of natural and historical interest.

rooms	7 doubles/twins.
price	€ 50.
meals	Breakfast € 5; dinner € 12.
closed	Rarely.
directions	From Vila Real N322 past Casa de Mateus for Sabrosa. At S. Martinho do Anta; right onto N322 2 for Gouvinhas. After town on for 1.5km; house signed on right.

Fernando Albuquerque

tel	+351 259 323121
fax	+351 259 326553
e-mail	casa.mateus@mail.telepac.pt

map 1   entry 27

Casa de Casal de Loivos

Casal de Loivos, 5085-010 Pinhão, Vila Real

One of the best views in this book – and anywhere! Built in 1658, this northern manor has been home to the Sampayos since 1733. The house is in the village, yet so placed that from the front you see no other dwelling, only the river Douro far below, winding its way through steep hills terraced with vineyards. It is a marvellous sight and every room opens to it. Tradition, comfort and gentility are the hallmarks here. Manuel is a truly old-fashioned, charming gentleman; he speaks perfect English and usually sports a cravat – this is a place where you dress for dinner. Traditional meat and fish dishes are created from old family recipes, and are always excellent. The dining room is simply beautiful, dominated by the large communal table – Manuel calls it "English-inn style". There is a comfortable sitting room which opens onto the terrace, below which is the pool and another terrace. The view-filled bedrooms are gorgeous, elegantly furnished and have good bathrooms. Fortified by good food and wine, well cared for by Manuel and his staff of nine, and able to watch the interplay of light, land and water for miles and miles, you'll feel somewhere halfway between earth and heaven.

rooms	6 doubles/twins.
price	€ 89; single € 69.
meals	Dinner € 22, on request.
closed	Christmas & January.
directions	From Pinhão to Alijó; 1st right & up through vineyards until Casal de Loivos. House on right at end of village.

Manuel Bernardo de Sampayo

tel	+351 254 732149
fax	+351 254 732149
e-mail	casadecasaldeloivos@ip.pt

Casa do Visconde de Chanceleiros

Largo da Fonte, Chanceleiros-Covas do Douro, 5085-201 Pinhão, Vila Real

This house has everything in abundance: big comfortable beds, squashy armchairs, lovely bathrooms, thick fluffy towels, great views, space inside and out, and friendly hosts and dogs. Kurt and Ursula's home is a classic granite and white manor house on the edge of a hillside village, with terraces on one side. Wide granite steps lead down to the terrace where there is a large pool with a long-roofed *cabana* furnished with sofa, stereo and tables. The house is tasteful and stylish, informal yet not over-casual. Your hosts are very welcoming, and so, too, is housekeeper Adelaide; she has been there 30 years. "We live with our guests, that's the difference," says Ursula. There are lots of warm colours inside, with furniture a mix of antique and modern; in the large colour-themed bedrooms are beautiful hand-painted furniture and beds. These rooms are rather like big bed-sitting rooms, and one is on two floors, ideal for a family. Breakfasts are feasts, and don't miss the splendid three-course dinners. All this and masses to do: ping-pong, pool, squash, billiards, boules, sauna and jacuzzi.

rooms	9 doubles/twins.
price	€95–€110; single €90.
meals	Lunch €20; dinner, with wine, €30, on request.
closed	Rarely.
directions	House signed from Pinhão.

Kurt & Ursula Böcking

tel	+351 254 730190
fax	+351 254 730199
web	www.chanceleiros.com

map 2   entry 29

Casa de Vilarinho de São Romão

Lugar da Capela, Vilarinho de São Romão, 5060-630 Sabrosa, Vila Real

This is a beautiful combination of old and new, of warm, sunny colours, light and space, the result of an excellent refurbishment of a 17th-century house overlooking the Pinhão valley, with a 1462 chapel at the entrance. Cristina's ancestors came to Portugal from Holland in the 18th century, and are an established port-wine family. She gave up teaching art to concentrate on the house, then a ruin; later she turned her attention to the vineyards around. The mood is light and airy, with pale wooden floors strewn with kilims and rugs, white walls, enormous rooms, grand paintings, fine antiques. The lounge is huge and comfortable, with large yellow sofas and lots of wood. Breakfast is generous, and includes fresh juice and fruit from the farm. One of the bedrooms has twin brass beds, rugs and a stone window seat, another a Dona Maria bed. White walls, bright curtains and polished wooden floors work beautifully together. Outside is a shaded terrace, and there's an inner gravelled courtyard with a pond. All this, lovely walks around the vineyards and fruit trees and, always, those long views across the Pinhão valley.

rooms	6 doubles/twins.
price	€ 75; single € 60; family room € 87.
meals	Dinner € 20, by arrangement.
closed	Christmas.
directions	From Vila Real to Pinhão through Sabrosa; in Vilarinho de São Romão, you will see granite gateway & chapel on left. Through gate.

Cristina van Zeller

tel	+351 259 930754
fax	+351 259 930754
e-mail	vilarinho@pax.jazznet.pt
web	www.casadevilarinho.com

Quinta do Real

Matosinhos, 5400 Chaves, Vila Real

You would travel far to find as elegant a building or as wonderful a rural setting as the Quinta do Real. The façade is a masterpiece of understated elegance. Long and low, it looks somehow gentle – the feminine touch perhaps, for it was built in 1697 for the Viscountess of Rio Maior. You pass through the entrance portal, topped by a granite cross, to enter a cobbled courtyard. We would choose a room in the main house with views across the valley, probably the master bedroom, but they all are large (except the attic room), spotlessly clean and prettily decorated with good-looking antiques. The other rooms are in outbuildings facing the patio; these are more basic but have more privacy. Back in the house is a cosy sitting room with a woodburning stove and another much larger one with a minstrels' gallery. The dining room is a delightful space, too; it has a chandelier, single table and a tallboy brimming with old china and glass. Your hosts are the charming Dona Celeste, who has lived here all her life, and her son Ramiro; he recently left a city career to dedicate himself to the house. There are a pool and barbecue outside, and horse-riding can be arranged.

rooms	10 doubles/twins.
price	€ 55–€ 65; single € 50–€ 55.
meals	Packed lunch € 17. Restaurants nearby.
closed	Rarely.
directions	From Vidago towards Loivos, then right for Quinta do Real. Through forest to village of Matosinhos: through village, then follow signs to Quinta.

Ramiro José Guerra

tel	+351 276 966253
fax	+351 276 965240

map 2   entry 31

Quinta da Mata

Estrada de Valpaços, 5400 Chaves, Vila Real

Filinto found this 17th-century Trás-os-Montes house in ruins and completely restored it, keeping nearly all the original features. He has made his ideals a reality and is endearingly enthusiastic about his home and this region's people and their food. For breakfast try miniature pasties, home-made bread, local Chaves ham and perhaps some smoked sausage. For dinner he may suggest kid or a delicious *cozido* (thick stew) and will certainly encourage you to try the wine from Valpaços. Quinta da Mata's bedrooms are as special as your host. The craftsmanship of the wooden floors and ceilings perfectly sets off the walls of dressed stone and hand-painted tiles; Arraiolos rugs, crocheted bedcovers, good repro beds and cut flowers lend warmth to large spaces. You might choose the Presidential suite which has an office/library, or the Imperial which is more private and has a whirlpool bath. There are two tennis courts, a sauna, free use of bikes and walks through the thickly wooded slopes of the Brunheiro mountains. "Filinto is charm itself," said our inspector, who has marvellous memories of afternoon tea with him at a table groaning under cheese, jam, doughnuts and cake.

rooms	6 doubles/twins/suites.
price	€55–€70; single €50–60; suite €64–€75.
meals	Dinner €10–€15.
closed	Rarely.
directions	Just outside Chaves; N213 to Valpaços, through Nantes. Quinta signed.

Filinto Moura Morais

tel	+351 276 340030
fax	+351 276 340038
e-mail	quinta.mata@netc.pt

Solar das Arcas

Arcas, 5340-031 Macedo de Cavaleiros, Bragança

In a forgotten, wine-growing corner of Portugal this lovely mansion has dignified the centre of the village of Arcas for over 300 years. The owners are direct descendants of Manuel Pessanha of Genoa, who came to teach the Portuguese the art of navigation. The house lies at the centre of a large estate of fruit orchards and olive groves. The pool is set in a walled courtyard. The main house is beautifully proportioned; carved mouldings surround windows and doors while the family coat of arms above the portal reminds you that this is a noble house – as do the imposing private chapel, *sala de piano*, ancient panelled ceilings – one octagonal – and stone staircase. "Cosy privacy" is how the brochure (correctly) describes the suites and apartments (the latter in outbuildings). There are very comfy sofas and superb antique beds. Food? Forgive us for quoting the Arcas brochure again: "You will feel that you belong to a real Portuguese family when you sit on a footstool savouring a glass of wine and nibbling at a piece of a smoked delicacy before the fireplace where iron vessels boil and the revolving plate grills simple, but first-rate meals". And the *vinho* is included in the price.

rooms	2 suites; 4 apartments.
price	Suite for 2-4, €74-€120; Imperial suite for 2, €100; apts for 2 €70.
meals	Lunch/dinner with wine, €25-€30, by arrangement.
closed	Rarely.
directions	From Bragança, IP4 for Vila Real & O Ponto-20. Exit for Macedo de Cavaleiros, then right on N15 for Zoio. After 1.7km, left via Ferreira to Arcas. House in village centre.

Maria Francisca Pessanha Machado

tel	+351 278 400010
fax	+351 278 401230
e-mail	solardasarcas@mail.telepac.pt

map 2   entry 33

CENTRAL PORTUGAL

"There's nothing under Heaven so blue
That's fairly worth the travelling to."

ROBERT LOUIS STEVENSON

Quinta da Ponte
Faia, 6300-095 Guarda

Just a short drive from Guarda, at the edge of the Serra da Estrêla and beside an old Roman bridge that crosses the river Mondego is an elegant 17th-century manor. The main façade is what first holds the eye; at one end is the Quinta's private chapel and next to it, a granite portal that leads to an inner courtyard. The dining room is in what was once the stable block – the granite feeding troughs have been kept as a feature but you will eat your (generous) breakfast from a china plate. Choose between a room in the old house or a modern apartment looking across the pool to the park beyond. Rooms are light (French windows on two sides), tiled, decorated in greens and pinks and each has a sitting room with hearth. Furniture is a mix of old and new and the feeling throughout is of unfolding history. There is a second, larger sitting room in a modern building next to the apartments. Here bedrooms maintain the period feel with lovely carved wooden beds. Do explore the walks along the river and the beautiful and well-designed garden that combines the natural with the neatly-clipped.

rooms	2 doubles/twins, 5 apartments.
price	€85, single €72; apt, for 2, €92.
meals	Lunch/dinner available locally.
closed	October-Easter, except New Year & Carnival.
directions	From Lisbon on IP5; exit 26 onto EN16 for Porto da Carne. House signed to right; follow road down to river & house (signed 'Turismo de Habitação').

Sociedade Turistica Historia e Jardins, LDA

tel	+351 271 926126
fax	+351 271 926839
e-mail	quintadaponte@oninet.pt
web	www.quintadaponte.com

map 2   entry 34

Quinta da Timpeira
Penude, 5100-718 Lamego, Viseu

A modern-looking home close to the Sanctuary of Nossa Senhora dos Remédios, an important pilgrimage site; many climb the 700 steps on their knees and countless miracles are attributed to Our Lady. You will be well looked after here by Francisco, an optometrist, and Isabel, a civil engineer. The house is bordered by a crisp, topiaried box hedge and below are terraces with pool, tennis court, fruit trees and four hectares of vines. Opposite are the Meadas mountains and behind are vineyards which supply the nearby Raposeira sparkling wine factory. The house is unfussy and, while the bedrooms are not particularly large, they are neatly decorated with good quality furniture and wooden or iron beds. Floors are strewn with rugs, and bathrooms convey a smartness despite grey tiles. The sitting/dining room is modern and unusual with a long curved wall – there are great views from its enormous window and balcony. Here you can have a traditional Portuguese dinner with Timpeira and other wines included. There's a small 'shop' downstairs where you can buy local handicrafts and you'll find a games room, bar and wine cellar, too.

rooms	7 doubles/twins.
price	€ 65; single € 53.
meals	Lunch/dinner with wine € 18, by arrangement.
closed	Rarely.
directions	From Lamego N2 for Viseu. Quinta is 2.5km after Raposeira sparkling wine factory, on left.

José Francisco Gomes Parente

tel	+351 254 612811
fax	+351 254 615176
e-mail	geral@quintadatimpeira.com

Casa Campo das Bizarras

Rua da Capela 76, Fareja, 3600-271 Castro Daire, Viseu

First impressions are deceptive, because from the road you see only the back of the house – but as you enter the garden, the lovely old granite façade is revealed. The garden and orchard are a sheer delight, the joint passions of Marina, a retired science teacher. She is an excellent hostess, and clearly loves what was her grandfather's house. It has bags of genuine rustic character, with walls of great blocks of stone, assorted tile and wooden floors, and wooden beams and ceilings. Some bedrooms are in the main house including the double with a beautifully grand antique bed (see photo) but most are in outbuildings. Some have kitchenettes hidden behind wooden doors, so the country character is maintained yet you can still make your own meals. (Or buy a fresh trout and grill it on the barbecue.) Public rooms are small and full of old domestic and rural-abilia: the lounge is upstairs and has a leather sofa, fireplace, big beams and ceramics on display; the reading room is downstairs, where there's a bar and pool table. It's all very cosy and there are plenty of places in which to sit and relax, outside and in.

rooms	5 doubles/twins; 4 self-catering apartments.
price	€60–€65; single €48–€53. Apartment for 2, €434–€466 per week, for 4 €628–€660 per week.
meals	Lunch/dinner €16, by arrangement.
closed	November–29 December.
directions	From Castro Daire to Fareginha. In Fareja left at sign for 'Turismo Rural'. Past church, up narrow cobbled lane, Bizarras on right.

Marina Rodrigues Moutinho

tel	+351 232 386107
fax	+351 232 382044
e-mail	casa.das.bizarras@mail.telepac.pt
web	www.casa-das-bizarras.web.pt

map 1   entry 36

Casa Grande de Casfreires

Ferreira de Aves, 3560-043 Sátão, Viseu

Annette has lead an extraordinary life and it's fun to share her awe-inspiring manor house. She runs the place with her son, Francisco, and looks after her two teenage grandchildren and her visitors with the same kindness. The sitting room has an enormous granite fireplace and photographs from Annette's past: of her as a child with her family in Phnom Phen, as a young woman shooting in Africa (the trophies are dotted around the room) and in France, in a classic car. The house and its outbuildings have been cleverly converted from cow sheds to luxury apartments, from pigsty to sparkling bathroom. There are now seven apartments (each with two bedrooms) plus three delightful rooms in the main house. The bedrooms have high doorways and ceilings, window seats, stripped wooden floors and crisp white linen. Views stretch down across fields and woodland to the valley below. The house, built in 1753, manages to combine a stately home atmosphere with the modern world. Some of the bathrooms have massage baths and power showers. Annette spoils you with home-made scones, hand-made chestnut jam and freshly picked nuts for breakfast. Wonderful.

rooms	3 doubles/twins; 7 self-catering apartments.
price	€ 75; apartments € 100.
meals	Lunch/dinner by arrangement.
closed	Occasionally.
directions	From Viseu, N229 to Sátão. Follow signs to Lamas de Ferreira & on to Casfreires.

SR Francisco Oliva

tel	+351 914 030807
e-mail	casa-grande@casfreires-oliva.com
web	www.casfreires-oliva.com

Quinta da Comenda
3660-404 São Pedro do Sul, Viseu

The lovely group of buildings is softened by a rampant camellia which lends swathes of colour when in flower. Lovers of organic wine may have heard of Quinta da Comenda; it exports its prize-winning whites and rosés all over the world. What you probably won't have heard is that the first king of Portugal, Dom Afonso Enriques, did battle nearby, broke a leg and was forced to stay at his uncle's place, the Quinta da Comenda. It later passed into the hands of the Order of Malta, hence the cross above the main entrance. Guest rooms match expectations after such an impressive arrival: polished parquet floors, elegant antique beds and pretty tiles in the bathroom. Lounge and dining room double up in a huge *salão* which leads to the old wine cellar, and you are treated to a real feast at the breakfast table. Little details such as the fruit basket and bottled water in your room show how much the da Rocha family care. Wander down to the river and a Roman bridge, through the vineyards and orchards, stock up on wine and find time to chat with your charming hosts. On most Saturdays in summer there are wedding parties; the ivy-clad chapel is to one end of the courtyard. *Minimum stay two nights.*

rooms	6 doubles/twins; 1 self-catering apartment for 4.
price	€75; single €67; apt €750 weekly.
meals	Breakfast €5. Restaurants nearby.
closed	Rarely.
directions	From Viseu, IP5 for S. Pedro do Sul on N16. A few km before S. Pedro follow 'Agro Turismo' sign; Quinta on left, signed.

Maria Laura Cardoso da Rocha

tel	+351 226 179889
fax	+351 226 183491
e-mail	quintadacomenda@hotmail.com
web	www.quintadacomenda.com

map 1   entry 38

Estalagem Casa D'Azurara
Rua Nova 78, 3530 Mangualde, Viseu

In a quiet corner of a sleepy town Casa D'Azurara is a perfect place to unwind and be pampered. This manor house was built by the Counts of Mangualde in the 17th century, added to at the end of the 19th century and renovated to create a small, luxurious hotel. There are two guest sitting rooms downstairs; one has an enormous old granite hearth, the other high French windows with draped and flounced curtains. There are framed etchings, potted palms, books, cut flowers and a good choice of fabric on chairs and sofas. Carpeted corridors (a lift if you need it) lead to the rooms, where furnishing is antique and repro; rich fabrics are used for bedspreads and curtains. Our choice would be suite-like 206; it has a sloping ceiling, Dona Maria beds and double French windows. Breakfast includes a choice of breads, cheeses and cold meats while the dinner menu has a strong regional bias; there are interesting fish dishes and a speciality is duck. Don't miss the gardens – magnolia, hortensias and camellia are an amazing size. The staff are caring and can organise wine tastings at nearby *adegas*. A place that successfully welcomes business people and travellers alike.

rooms	15: 14 doubles/twins, 1 suite.
price	€87–€97; suite €114–€129; single €79–€89.
meals	Lunch from €15; dinner from €20.
closed	Rarely.
directions	From Porto, IP5 for Guarda. Exit for Mangualde. House in town centre, signed. (Do not confuse with 2nd modern Estalagem at town entrance).

Aldina Salgado

tel	+351 232 612010
fax	+351 232 622575
e-mail	casa.azurara@esoterica.pt
web	www.casa-azurara.pt

Quinta do Rio Dão

3440-464 Santa Comba Dão, Viseu

The setting is a dream, with the house almost hidden in a stand of old oaks right on the bank of the river Dão at the very point where it opens out to form a small lagoon. Pieter and Juliette, wonderfully friendly hosts both, came across the farmhouse when it stood in ruins and have sensitively restored it and the neighbouring buildings in traditional Beira style. They offer you the choice of a room, an apartment or a whole house: the common threads are a beautiful use of wood, big verandas and captivating prospects down towards the river. Pieter and Juliette have married traditional Portugal with a clean, uncluttered (and Dutch) approach to space: there is nothing too showy to detract from the sheer pleasure of being here. In summer, life is spent mostly outdoors; breakfast on the veranda to birdsong, relax at night with the lights of nearby Santa Comba Dão reflected in the water. Rooms are marvellous value. There are canoes, a rowing boat and a windsurfer for guests to use, and pets can be housed, but not in the rooms. Our inspector loved her stay: "In a word, idyllic". This is just the place for a really energising holiday and children would love it here, too.

rooms	4 doubles/twins; 2 self-catering apartments for 2-4; 3 cottages for 4-8.
price	€50-€60; apartment €50 €60; cottage €90-€180.
meals	Available locally.
closed	Rarely.
directions	From Lisbon, A1 for Porto. After Coimbra, IP3 for Viseu. 500m before Santa Comba Dão turn to Vimieiro. Follow sign 'Agro Turismo' for 4.5km to Quinta.

Pieter & Juliette Gruppelaar-Spierings

tel	+351 232 892784
fax	+351 232 892372
e-mail	quinta@quintadoriodao.com
web	www.quintadoriodao.com

map 4   entry 40

Casa O Nascer Do Sol

Vale da Carvalha, Carvalho, 3360-034 Penacova, Viseu

Lucy and Hans are delightful hosts and cannot do enough for you. They are Belgian, have lived in Portugal for two years and speak fluent Portuguese as well as French, English, German and Dutch. You'll be greeted with a bottle of local bubbly and Hans can take you on trips to wine cellars and around the local area. The shuttered bedrooms are all beige, simple and comfortable, with dark wooden beds, fans and side tables. The house is modern with a lovely beamed lounge/dining room; Flemish paintings, old antiques and leather sofas give a grand but comfortable feel. This is a peaceful village so you can eat outside to birdsong. Breakfasts are generous and you're encouraged to make yourself sandwiches for lunch – locals pop in daily to drop off the freshest produce. Hans will also take you to a typical, local restaurant on your first evening if you like, and give advice on good treks from the house. The garden has a small pool, potted geraniums and palms and there are pines, olive trees and eucalyptus all around. If you want to be truly looked after, this is the place to come. *Minimum stay three nights.*

rooms	6 doubles.
price	€36–€46.
meals	Restaurants nearby.
closed	Rarely.
directions	Exit A1 Lisbon-Porto at Coimbra-Norte; IP3 for Viseu & Guarda; exit 10 for Penacova N235 Luso & Bussaco. Hans will meet you to guide you the 15km to Vale de Carvalha.

Hans & Lucy Ghijs de Voghel

tel	+351 239 476871
fax	+351 239 476872
e-mail	npp72198@mail.telepac.pt
web	www.casaonascerdosol.com

Casa das Ribas

Lugar do Castelo, 4520 Santa Maria da Feira, Aveiro

Opposite a castle in woods above the town you walk into the enormous entrance hall and enter another age. Over a double pony-cart hangs a large family coat of arms: this is a stately home replete with chandeliers and beautiful furnishings. The atmosphere, however, is easy, and Maria Carmina and her family enjoy having guests and speaking English with them. The bedrooms are traditional and luxurious with a selection of Dom José and Edwardian beds and modern bathrooms. The suite is more contemporary and very attractive, with no fewer than seven windows overlooking the gardens. The separate, and more rustic Casa do Caseiro has a huge double bedroom: "the most gorgeous holiday cottage", to quote our inspector. You breakfast in the main house in the old kitchen near the vast fireplace. There are several drawing rooms, including the *sala da musica*, with grand piano, grand sofa and fireplace, and there's a beautiful dining room which opens onto the gardens. Maria has the greenest fingers and this place is a must if you love gardens; parts are park-like, with hydrangeas, rhododendrons, roses, palms and cedars. There's also the library, a games room and a beautiful 16th-century chapel.

rooms	6: 5 doubles/twins, 1 suite; 1 self-catering house for 4.
price	€ 60–€ 75; single € 50; suite € 75. House € 100.
meals	Available locally.
closed	Rarely.
directions	Exit Lisboa & Porto m'way at Feira & follow signs for Castelo; you can see castle in trees on way into Feira; house next to castle.

Maria Carmina Vaz de Oliveira
tel	+351 256 373485
fax	+351 256 374481

map 1   entry 42

Casa de Sol Nascente

Rua de Alagoa, Taipa, Requeixo, 3800-881 Aveiro, Aveiro

East meets west in 'the house of the rising sun'. The architecture is the work of Ian's Japanese wife Chizu, an artist whose beautifully exotic paintings hang in many rooms (and in the Tokyo National Gallery, too). You enter to a column of glass around which curves a flight of stairs; large windows the light floods in. Some walls are curved, too, and cast graduated shadows. Chizu is fond of the roundness of the place: "curves bring nature into the living room and soften the mood," she says. The bedrooms contain a successful blend of pieces from around the world; the suites, Acacia and Bamboo, are particularly well furnished. Chizu and Ian are easy and well travelled (he worked in many parts of the world before settling here). They are excellent hosts and effortlessly create a gentle mood and a family atmosphere – this is a great place to come with children. Meals from Chizu are superb and span a wide range of Portuguese and Japanese cooking; in the summer they do excellent barbecues. Snacks are on request. Nearby are the famous Aveiro lagoons, full of wildlife, and the sea is 10km away. A wonderfully welcoming and tranquil place.

rooms	4: 2 doubles/twins, 2 suites; apartment for 6.
price	€45; suite €78. Apt €930 per week.
meals	Lunch/dinner by arrangement.
closed	Rarely.
directions	A1; EN235 for Aveiro; immed. right to Mamodeiro; at 1st café, 1st junc. right to Requeixo. On to Taipa. Road bends down to right; at bend take smaller road going up on right; last house, 800m.

Ian M Arbuckle

tel	+351 234 933597
fax	+351 234 933598
e-mail	arbuckle@mail.telepac.pt
web	www.solnascente.aveiro.co.pt

Solar do Ervedal

Rua Dr. Francisco Brandão 12, 3405-063 Ervedal da Beira, Coimbra

Though architectural styles have come and gone, this noble 500-year-old residence, built in granite, has never left the hands of the descendants of Diogo Braz Pinto. High walls surround the estate and you enter through elegant wrought-iron gates – once within, the village seems another world. A cobbled courtyard with pots of geraniums fronts the house; behind are acres of organically farmed orchards and a stand of 200-year-old oaks. Guest rooms are in the south wing, the oldest part of the manor. The house is grand: the large sitting room has an unusual octagonal ceiling and Gothic door arches of local granite; two burgundy sofas are pulled up to the hearth. It's good to see a chessboard taking pride of place while the TV is hidden in a cupboard. The dining room is just as delightful and eating in is recommended: roast duck with rice is a speciality, desserts are delicious and wines are local. Bedrooms are grand, with ornate beds and other fine antique furniture, set off by parquet floors, stuccoed ceilings and window seats. The present Viscountess Maria Helena is a kind, gracious hostess – you'll be reluctant to leave.

rooms	6: 5 doubles/twins/family, 1 suite.
price	€90; single €80; family €115; suite €125.
meals	Lunch/dinner €17, by arrangement.
closed	November & Christmas.
directions	Just before Oliveira do Hospital centre (off N1 / Coimbra-Guarda), right just after VW garage to Ervedal da Beira. 16km to village. Solar signed from village centre.

Maria Helena de Albuquerque

tel	+351 238 644283
fax	+351 238 641133
e-mail	solardoervedal@mail.telepac.pt

map 1   entry 44

Quinta da Fontinha

Apartado 80, Espariz, 3420 Tabua, Coimbra

A relaxed new hostelry, run by a young Dutch couple, in Portugal's green heart. Choose between brand-new rooms downstairs, and 'old' rooms on the upper floors. These, with their wooden planks and original doors, have more character, but you do have to share shower rooms and toilets. All are light and a good size, the furniture is solidly straightforward and the paintwork spotless. Ground-floor rooms, painted yellow, have their own bathrooms. There's a comfortable lounge upstairs, and a roof terrace with dreamy mountain views. Breakfast is served in the barn next door – and, one Sunday a month, a delicious Chinese lunch is cooked by a Chinese cook and attended by up to 30 guests and ex-pats, many of whom are Dutch. To the front of the hotel are olive groves and gardens, jollied up with geraniums but still somewhat overgrown; beyond, fields and woods. There is a tiny pool, too, perfect for dips on a hot day. Walking country is all around, and there's canoeing on the rivers, and swimming. We recommend the Quinta as a stopover en route to the coast: it is wonderfully near the N-17 to Coimbra though not a hum of traffic – you could be miles from anywhere. *Minimum stay two nights.*

rooms	15: 14 doubles/twins, 1 single.
price	€90–€120 (2 nights); €280–€380 per week.
meals	Lunch 1st Sunday of month. Restaurants near by.
closed	Rarely.
directions	From A1 Porto-Lisbon, exit Coimbra Norte. Then IP3 for Viseu, into IC7 for Guarda. Exit for Tabua. In Espariz, left at sign for Tabua, downhill. 1st house on right.

Roberto & Luisa Leijgraaff

tel	+351 235 713 668
fax	+351 235 713 637
e-mail	info@quintadafontinha.com
web	www.quintadafontinha.com

Quinta das Mestras

Nogueira do Cravo, 3400 Oliveira do Hospital, Coimbra

A stream – dipped into by birds – runs between the rambling stone buildings of the *quinta* and the *cabanes*. The old farmstead in its hillocky seven acres is surrounded by pine forests and olive groves; the Sierra da Estrela rises nobly beyond. Dutch-born Rob and Australian Leondra – he a designer and cartoonist, she a translator – are engaging hosts whose B&B is as vibrant as they are. Bedrooms are named after the colour of each of their delightfully sloped wooden ceilings: Green, Yellow, Pink. Green is the nicest, with its own terracotta bathroom and ochre-painted wrought-iron beds pushed cosily together. Pancakes, omlettes, fruit – something different is served for breakfast each day (included in the B&B price), served on suitably rustic plates on a shady terrace or in the decoratively cluttered kitchen. Up on the hill, sharing a bathroom, are two self-catering *cabanes* – simple and private. You are two miles from the shops and restaurants of the charming little town of Oliveira do Hospital; river canoeing and swimming are not much further, and fabulous walks start from the door. A fun, arty place to stay in one of Portugal's prettiest green corners.

rooms	1 doubles; 1 twin; 2 cabins.
price	€ 32–€ 45; € 195–€ 305 week. Cabins € 29; € 195 week; use of kitchen € 10.
meals	Breakfast € 5. Dinner by arrangement.
closed	Rarely.
directions	From Coimbra towards Ceira; N17 for Oliveira do Hospital. Before Oliveira, exit for Nogueira do Gravo & Bobadela. Between Nogueira & Bobadela. Just off road, signed.

Leondra Wesdorp

tel	+351 238 602988
fax	+351 238 602989
e-mail	wesdorp@pandaline.pt
web	www.pandaline.pt/qtamestras

map 4   entry 46

Quinta da Geía

Aldeia das Dez, 3400-214 Oliveira do Hospital, Coimbra

Aldeia das Dez in the foothills of the Serra da Estrela is an old hamlet to which the 21st century seems only to have given a passing glance. From the outside you'd never guess that the house is several hundred years old: Dutch Frenkel de Greeuw and Fir have completely renovated the place. Life at Quinta da Geía centres on the lively bar and restaurant. It has stained wooden tables and chairs, bright tablecloths, paintings by local artists and is well frequented by the local folk who obviously approve of the cooking: Frenkel describes it as "trad Portuguese with a difference", the difference being an Italian/French slant in the preparation of sauces and veg. Once a week bread is baked in the original brick oven. Bedrooms are large, light and functional; they have pine floors, interesting angles and are beautifully finished. A suite or apartment would be perfect for families. Your hosts have mapped out the best walks in the area – follow ancient (Roman) pathways through forests of oak and chestnut. An exceptional place, now with two large conference rooms. *Minimum stay in apartments one week in summer, three nights rest of year.*

rooms	15 doubles; 1 suite; 3 self-catering apartments for 4-6.
price	€55-€82; single €45-€75; suite €80-€100. Apts €95-€117 per day; €570-€700 week.
meals	Lunch/dinner €22.
closed	2-22 January.
directions	From Coimbra, IP3 to intersection with IC6. 10km before Oliveira, at Vendas de Galizes, right signed 'Hotel Rural' for 14km.

Fir Tiebout

tel	+351 238 670010
fax	+351 238 670019
e-mail	quintadageia@mail.telepac.pt
web	www.quintadageia.com

Telhado Visto

rua de verde wood, Sãomão, Lamento, Coimbra

There are no signs of the passage of the Roman, Carthaginian, French and British armies who trod these lands in such deadly military earnest. No vestige of the once-mighty Portuguese Empire remains. No pillars claw the sky and stand proud against the winds of change. All that you can now see is this – this humble heap of charred stones where once a peasant family lived and toiled. No bones are made – it is simple living at its luxurious simplest. Discard the peripherals you usually take with you on holiday and equip yourself with suitcases of imagination and resilience. You might add such luxuries as plastic sheeting, a paraffin heater, camping bed, torch. Or just bring all your camping kit and pretend that you are outside. Your views over this lush valley will nevertheless be framed by old windows. Your views of the night sky will be framed by charred beams – more than most camp-sites can provide and unusual in this over-developed world. And though your view of Portugal will be forever tarnished remember that it is better to travel hopefully than to arrive.

rooms	1 self-catering house, for 10.
price	€ 10 (up to 10 people)
meals	Fungus and moss.
closed	Dry season.
directions	From Sãomão, follow the moss until horse-jumps; dive over head first and you're there.

Ináçio Maria Maria de Maria Maria de Maria
tel   +351 7777777
e-mail   mossyandwoody@verywild.pt
web   www.arcwenearlythereyet.com

Casa da Azenha Velha

Caceira de Cima, 3080 Figueira da Foz, Coimbra

Once a flour mill (*azenha*), this large house is now much more: the decorative flourishes above doors and windows and large rooms suggest a grand history. After Maria de Lourdes and her dog have met you, you will find that the grounds teem with other creatures: deer, ostriches, cows, horses and peacocks. The bedrooms and apartment are separate from the main house and have been decorated with great attention to detail and colour; even tiles match the fabrics and there are large sunken baths. It is excellent value. You breakfast in the large kitchen of the main house; rail-sleepers support the roof-bricks, an original and attractive feature. Here too is a snug living room with leather sofas, a hearth and lots of ornaments. There's a large lounge in the old stable block with an honesty bar. The Azenha is perfect for family visits: as well as the animals, which children will love, there are plenty of board games, snooker table, pool, tennis court and six horses to be ridden. Not far from the main house is the new, rustic-style Azenha restaurant where you eat regional and international dishes.

rooms	5 doubles; 1 apartment for 4.
price	€ 70; apartment € 110.
meals	Restaurant on farm.
closed	Rarely.
directions	From Coimbra, N111 for Figueira da Foz. Shortly before Figuiera turn towards Caceira, then immed. left following signs 'Turismo Rural'. After 2km right for 500m, then right again. House on left.

Maria de Lourdes Nogueira
tel +351 233 425041
fax +351 233 429704

Quinta das Lagrimas

Santa Clara, Apart. 5053, 3041-901 Coimbra

Quinta das Lagrimas has a place among the most remarkable hostelries in Portugal, perhaps in Europe. The Palace is 300 years old but was rebuilt after a fire a century ago. Wellington stayed here and was captivated by the place and the legend that the tears (*lagrimas*) of the name were those shed by Dona Inês when put to the dagger by the knights of King Alfonso. Come to see 10 acres of wonderful gardens – some of which have been taken up by the golf school; many species have been brought from all over the world, and two giant sequoias were a gift from the Iron Duke himself (hence *Wellingtonia*). The elegance of the double sweep of staircase leading up to the main front is mirrored within. The dining room is stuccoed, panelled and chandeliered; dignitaries are international but the the food is Portuguese and accompanied by fine wines from Lagrimas's large cellars. Bedrooms are fit for kings (a number have stayed here) but ask for one in the old house rather than the annexe: elegant and deeply luxurious with rich fabrics, vast beds and marbled bathrooms. There is a colonnaded swimming pool, a snooker room for a post-prandial game and interesting works of modern art.

rooms	39: 35 doubles/triples, 4 suites.
price	€ 149–€ 189; triple € 300; suite € 300–€ 375; single € 121–€ 152.
meals	Lunch/dinner € 35–€ 50.
closed	Rarely.
directions	Just outside Coimbra, behind 'Portugal dos Pequenitos', EN1 for Lisbon; right at hotel sign.

Mario Morais

tel	+351 239 802380
fax	+351 239 441695
e-mail	hotelagrimas@mail.telepac.pt
web	www.supernet.pt/hotelagrimas

map 3　entry 50

Casa Pombal

Rua das Flores 18, 3000-442 Coimbra

Pombal is the Portuguese for dovecote and this old townhouse is delightful. At the heart of Coimbra, among narrow streets on a hill close to the famous seat of learning, it is friendly, utterly unpretentious and will stir feelings of nostalgia for those student years. Four of the rooms have breathtaking views over the old city roofscape and down to the Mondego river. They are basic but very clean and comfortable; three have their own bathrooms, but sacrifice a little luxury for the sweeter pleasures of those views and the relaxed atmosphere created by the friendly Dutch owners, who are very willing to give lots of local information. It is better to book in advance, and single folk will especially enjoy this place, where they're bound to meet fellow travellers over breakfast (eggs, cereals, fresh juices and home-made jams) or in the small courtyard. Pets are allowed in rooms but not the common room or patio. Built on hills overlooking the river Mondego, Coimbra is a city to explore slowly; once capital of the (young) nation it is most famous for its very ancient university. Try to visit in term time when the students add so much life to the city.

rooms	10 doubles/twins, some sharing bathroom.
price	€38–€48; sharing bathroom, €30–€40; single €28–€48.
meals	Dinner €14, minimum 4 people.
closed	Mid-December–mid-February.
directions	In Coimbra follow signs 'Universidad' via Ave. Sá da Bandeira; towards Praça da Republica; last right before Praça, right onto Rua. Padre António Vieira. Park at end of street. If lost ask for Rua da Matemática.

Else Denninghoff Stelling

tel	+351 239 835175
fax	+351 239 821548

Casa do Cimo

Aldeia Nova do Cabo, 12, 6230-050 Fundão, Castelo Branco

Grand, gracious, grandiose… the Casa do Cimo is all these and more. The house, festooned with Virginia creeper, was built in 1578 and has belonged to the same noble family ever since. Much has happened here over the centuries, and you'll see the family coat of arms over the entrance, over the fireplace and embroidered in colour on the towels. This large, cream, granite building, sited at the top of the village, has superb views of the Serra da Estrela mountains behind. The dining room, sitting room and halls are all magnificent, with stone walls, large stone arches, vast fireplaces and wooden ceilings, and all superbly decorated. Most of the bedrooms are very grand, with high ceilings and beautifully crafted antique furniture. Breakfast is self-service in the lovely old kitchen, delicious with freshly squeezed orange juice and home-made jams. Outside is an attractive garden and a *tanque* – take a quick, cooling dip – fed by spring water. And you are yards from the cobbled streets of the village. Come for the grandeur, the views, the peace.

rooms	11: 10 doubles/twins, 1 suite.
price	€75; single €60; suite €100.
meals	Dinner €20, by arrangement.
closed	Rarely.
directions	From IP2 Castelo Branco-Guarda for Fundão. Through Fundão to old church, sign Aldeia Vona & Silvaras; to Silvaras; after 2km, right at sign for Aldeia Nova do Cabo. House on left in village.

Judite & Jõao da Câmara Vasconcelos Alvaiazere
tel +351 275 771431
fax +351 243 324991

map 4   entry 52

Casa do Castelo Novo

Rua Nossa Senhora das Graças - 7, 6230-160 Castelo Novo, Castelo Branco

A 17th-century home on the slopes of the Serra da Gardunha, an amphitheatre that leads down to the winding lanes of the village. The granite stonework front of this elegant house is deceptive: you cannot guess how the house is built up the steep rock, nor that the garden is at the level of the first floor. The ground floor is a sitting room for guests, where there are sofas, a wall of rock, and carpets from the Minho and Morocco. Up a wooden staircase and you find the main living room; here are sofas, a granite fireplace, bookcases cut into the stone walls, displays of ceramics, antiques and a shell-like wooden *maceira* ceiling. The dining/breakfast room is cosy, in 19th-century style. In the main house are a bedroom and suite, both with Dona Maria beds – the latter has the best view in the whole house, according to Alice. A few steps across the garden and you have a choice of a painted Alentejo double or romantic twins. Alice and Maunuel are very friendly and welcoming and prepare delicious Portuguese food. The garden is simple, flourishing... and what views!

rooms	4: 3 doubles/twins, 1 suite.
price	€ 40–€ 60; single € 37-45; suite € 60-70.
meals	Lunch/dinner € 15–€ 20, by arrangement.
closed	Rarely.
directions	IP2 to Fundão. Near Fundão, signs to Castelo. Enter on R. de São Brás; at Largo da Bica right along R. da Gardunha, around castle, till join R. Nossa Senhora das Graças; signs.

Alice Aleixo

tel	+351 275 561373
fax	+351 275 561373
e-mail	castelo.novo@clix.pt
web	www.castelonovo.web.pt

Casa do Outeiro

Largo Carvalho do Outeiro 4, 2440-128 Batalha, Leiria

This small modern guest house is right in the centre of Batalha, its hillside perch ensuring that some bedrooms have views across the town's rooftops to the colossal Abbey. The Abbey was built in gratitude for Dom João's victory over the Castilian army in 1385 (a battle that secured the independence of Portugal) and is a masterpiece of Portuguese Manueline art, its exterior all carved pinnacles, columns and buttresses; the innards, especially the cloisters, are exceptionally beautiful too. If you come to visit the Abbey do stay at Casa do Outeiro even if at first appearance it is a rather unexciting place. José and Odete are the best of hosts; both manage to combine careers in the town with attending to their guests. Their bedrooms are roomy and functional; all have modern pine furniture and own baths but their private terraces lift them into the 'special' league, and the wooden floors and ceilings add warmth. Most of the area to the rear of the building is given over to the swimming pool. The ever-helpful owners will advise you where to dine out and, in the morning, treat you to a generous breakfast that includes five or six home-made jams. Excellent value.

rooms	15: 10 doubles, 5 family rooms.
price	€ 40–€ 55; single € 40; family room € 55–€ 70.
meals	Restaurants nearby.
closed	Rarely.
directions	In Batalha, follow signs for centre. House signed.

José Victor Pereira Madeira

tel	+351 244 765806
fax	+351 244 765806
e-mail	geral@casadoouteiro.com
web	www.casadoouteiro.com

map 3   entry 54

Casa da Padeira

EN8 - S. Vicente 19, Alcobaça, 2460-711 Aljubarrota, Leiria

Casa da Padeira takes its name from the baker's wife of Aljubarrota who, so legend has it, single-handedly dispatched seven Spaniards. A frieze of *azulejos* (tiles) on the bar in the lounge shows her thwacking one of the septet into the bread oven. Several centuries on, a more gentle reception awaits you at this quiet guest house run by Lena and Nuno. The house is not old but the bedrooms on the first floor have an antique style thanks to ornately turned Bilros beds and furniture. The self-contained apartments (some with wheelchair access) are well furnished; bedrooms are a good size; sometimes there's an additional sofabed, and some of the bathrooms are brand new. The lounge has a wide stone fireplace for colder nights and capacious yellow-striped armchairs and sofa. You breakfast well at Padeira, with a selection of bread, cake, cheese and meat, and for further pleasure there is an excellent restaurant in nearby Aljubarrota. When you return after forays, visit the games room, with cheerful yellow-orange walls and pool table and other diversions. The garden has a pleasant sheltered swimming pool bordered by plants, with sunloungers, tables and chairs aplenty.

rooms	8 doubles/twins; 6 apartments for 2-6.
price	€ 50-€ 70; single € 40-€ 55. Apartments € 85-€ 120.
meals	Self-catering in apartments. Restaurant nearby.
closed	Rarely.
directions	Along EN8 from Alcobaça for Batalha. House signed on left after leaving Aljubarrota.

Lina Pacheco

tel	+351 262 505240
fax	+351 262 505241
e-mail	casadapadeira@mail.telepac.pt

A Colina Atlântica

Quinta das Maças, Travessa dos Melquites 3, Barrantes, 2500-621 Salir de Matos, Leiria

Meditation, tarot, reiki, communal meals... this is a house with its own special atmosphere and focus. Its 1950s exterior may look unprepossessing but the company is good and the mood informal. Ineke and her partner Ton, who have travelled a good deal in India and Asia, soon make you feel at home – this is a good place to come if you're travelling alone. The house's huge loft is now a beautiful meditation room with a wood-lined roof, cotton rugs and futons, where you can combine spiritual interests with more earthly pursuits. 'Guided meditation' – and breakfast – are included. If you'd like a knowledgeable escort, Ton will take you to the monasteries of Alcobaça and Batalha, to Óbidos and Nazaré. The bedrooms, in what once were the stables, have tiled floors and wooden ceilings; they are basic but comfortable. (There is even more basic accommodation in caravans out in the large garden!). There's no maid service, so you clean your own room. Most nights there are communal 'world cuisine' dinners in the dining room which opens onto the pleasant garden with tinkling chimes. A friendly place which works its magic on many levels.

rooms	2: 1 double, 1 single; 3 caravans for 1-3.
price	€ 40; single € 25; caravans € 25-€ 32.
meals	Dinner € 12 with wine, on request.
closed	November-April (open Christmas & New Year).
directions	From Caldas da Rainha for Alcobaça. After 6km, at Tornada, right to Barrantes. At end of village, fork left at sign to Valado; after 100m; right opp. new house. House 50m on left.

Ineke van der Wiele

tel	+351 262 877312
e-mail	info@a-colina-atlantica.com

map 3   entry 56

Casa do Casal do Pinhão

Bairro Sra. da Luz, 2510 Óbidos, Leiria

Not far from the medieval town of Óbidos, in pine forests and farmland, is this country retreat, a long modern house with bedrooms in a line overlooking the pool. It's a mixture of purpose-built-for-rural-tourism, family home and stud farm. Each 18th-century style bedroom has a different colour theme and Dona Maria beds with high headboards. The apartments here are large, very modern and Portuguese in style. In the mornings, climb out of bed, throw open the French windows, and take a dip in the pool set into the terrace below (there's also a shallow one for children). You'll hear only the birds singing and perhaps sheep or goats and you can see the famous arch-necked Lusitanian horses in stables nearby. There are pine, oak and eucalyptus trees near the house, and a shady pergola where you can take a drink from the 'honesty' bar. Breakfast is self-service and continental. Traditional Portuguese cooking is available in the evenings but there are interesting restaurants in the old streets of Óbidos. *Further two-bedroom apartments 1 km at neighbouring quinta.*

rooms	8 doubles/twins; 4 self-catering apartments for 2-4.
price	€ 60-€ 80. Apartments € 80 for 2; € 90 for 3; € 100 for 4.
meals	Restaurants nearby.
closed	Rarely.
directions	From Óbidos, EN8 to Caldas da Rainha & Tomar. Look for blue signs to house.

Maria Adelaide

tel	+351 262 959078
fax	+351 262 959078
e-mail	casal.pinhao@iol.pt
web	www.mundo.iol.pt/casal.pinhao/turismo

Casa de S. Thiago do Castelo

Largo de S. Thiago, 2510-106 Óbidos, Leiria

Don't miss Óbidos, cradled by its very old, 14th-century wall. It is a beguiling maze of narrow cobbled streets softened by blue and ochre pastel washes and romping stands of bougainvillaea and jasmine. There are cameo views at every turn. The 'house of St James' has been in the family for over a century, though it is more recently that Carlos decided to throw it open to guests. A cheery French housekeeper welcomes you in; from the outside you could not guess the extent of this old house. Decoration has been meticulously studied and carefully crafted. Bedrooms vary but their most memorable features are massively thick walls (some windows are large enough for *conversadeiros* – gossiping seats!) and dark wood ceilings. There are wrought-iron bedsteads, matching prints for curtains and bedspreads, swanky bathrooms and details that you'd only expect of a larger hotel, like logo-ed writing paper and envelopes. On one level is a small lounge with open hearth; down below is a bar (try a glass of the local cherry liqueur, *ginjinha*), a billiard room and, in the lee of the castle battlements, the most peaceful of patios for sitting out. Carlos enjoys exchanging anecdotes with his guests.

rooms	8 doubles/twins.
price	€ 85-€ 90; single € 70-€ 75.
meals	Good restaurants nearby.
closed	Rarely.
directions	Enter Óbidos through main gate. Continue to end of street. House on right, below castle.

Carlos Lopes

tel	+351 262 959587
fax	+351 262 959587

map 3   entry 58

Quinta de Santa Catarina

Rua Visconde da Palma d'Almeida, 2530-166 Lourinhã, Lisboa

If style, elegance, comfort and service are high on your list of hotel essentials then Quinta de Santa Catarina is your type of place. It was built in the 16th century, rebuilt in the 18th and embellished by various illustrious forebears of the Almeida Braga family; they even escaped collectivisation during the Revolution. The expanding suburbs of Lourinhã have brought new neighbours but the building still looks out across wooded grounds where the tallest of palm trees (you'll find them on the family coat of arms too) increase the sensation of coming across a genuine oasis. You may be met by a uniformed maid who will lead you to your room via elegant reception rooms where ancestral portraits, gilded mirrors and chandeliers, brilliant polished tables and dressers, candelabras and flowers would provide a wonderful backdrop for the grandest of weddings. That frisson of expectation is rewarded when the door of your room is pushed open and you are greeted by polished antique beds, dressers and occasional tables, more cut flowers, deep-pile carpets and captivating views out to the palm trees. Teresa teaches English and has a gift for making you feel immediately relaxed.

rooms	5 doubles/twins.
price	€75-€89; single €60-€77.
meals	Snacks by the pool. Available locally.
closed	24-25 December.
directions	From Lisbon, A8 north for Oporto. Exit at junc. 9 to Lourinhã. In Lourinhã, at r'bout with fountain, take Rua Adelino Amaro da Costa, past restaurant D. Sebastiao. Entrance on right.

Teresa Maria Palma de Almeida Braga

tel	+351 261 422313
fax	+351 261 414875
e-mail	quinta.santa.catarina@netc.pt

Casa Lido

Monte da Portelinha, Silveira, 6030-021 Fratel, Lisboa

This pretty cluster of Beira cottages is on the edge of a village frozen in time: old ladies wash lettuce at a shared tap and bake bread in an oven just opposite. Lise and Udo are English and German warm and kind; she is a designer, he a colour chemist; their talents are reflected in their gorgeous self-catering cottages. The biggest house, for four, has low, dark wooden ceilings, roughly-rendered white walls, chairs and carved beds made by a local carpenter to their own designs. All rooms are beautifully lit; even the fruit bowl has been artistically placed. The cottage, which sleeps two, has a spiral iron staircase, a wood-burning stove and views over soft countryside towards the river from both courtyard and terrace. The converted barn, also for two, has a mezzanine, a huge window and a flower-filled terrace with a pergola. All have kitchens or kitchenettes and there's a delightful walled pool to share. Lise can tell you everything you need to know, from when the bread and fish men come to the best local *festas*. If you don't feel like cooking, Udo is an excellent chef, generous with wine and garlic. *Occasional art & gourmet food weekends.*

rooms	3 self-catering houses.
price	€ 192–€ 560 per week. From € 60 per night. B&B also available.
meals	Dinner € 20–€ 30, with wine.
closed	Rarely.
directions	A1 Lisbon-Porto, exit 7 onto IP6. IP2-A23, exit 16 Silveira. Right Riscada-Juncal; under dual c'way; left at T-junc. for Riscada/Silveira. Pass Riscada exit; cont. until sign for Silveira. In village, follow road round to right; at end.

Lise & Udo Reppin

tel	+351 272 566393
mobile	+351 914 111469

map 3   entry 60

Quinta do Salvador do Mundo

2590-211 Sobral de Monte Agraço, Lisboa

The Quinta of the Saviour of the World once belonged to the bishopric of Évora and is a large farmhouse near a Roman-Gothic church of the same name. This is an area of vineyards, rolling hills and windmills, and the farm overlooks a vast valley with views to the Serra do Socorro (Wellington's 'redoubt' was on the hill opposite during the Peninsular War). The *quinta* has been stylishly rebuilt, a stunning blend of old and new. It has grand furniture, a Steinway, chandeliers, silver, family antiques and lots of glass and pine – all in a light and airy building. The furniture includes English, French, Portuguese and Indo-Portuguese pieces. Moroccan mosaic tables stand on a terrace outside the magnificent dining/breakfast room which has windows along one side and views of the valley and ruined church. Four bedrooms are in a separate building; they too are roomy and comfortable, each with antique beds and desks. Enjoy the luxury you'd expect from a top hotel, the grandeur of a *casa nobre* and a beautifully designed modern setting. Maria is gracious, friendly and well-travelled. *Five bedrooms in main house not generally available.*

rooms	9 doubles.
price	€97–€125; single €85–€115.
meals	Available locally.
closed	20 October–15 November.
directions	From A8 exit junc. 6, left at Pero Negro; left again, then right, follow signs for Salvador (7km from motorway).

Maria Teresa Sucena Paiva

tel	+351 261 943880
fax	+351 261 943199
e-mail	quintasalvador@ip.pt
web	www.quintasalvador.com

Pensão Residencial Sintra

Quinta Visconde de Tojal, Travessa dos Avelares, Nº 12, 2710-506 Sintra (S.Pedro), Lisboa

We loved the air of faded grandeur enveloping this family-run guest house. It was built on a thickly-wooded hillside as a viscount's summer retreat in the days when fashionable Sintra was a hill station to local and international gentry – and became a guest house just after the war. An original bannistered staircase winds up to the first- and second-floor bedrooms. These are enormous with high ceilings, wooden floors and endearingly dated furniture and fittings; it all has a distinctly out-of-time feel. Ask for one of the two rooms with mountain views. Downstairs is an enormous dining room/bar where snacks are normally available, but we'd prefer to sit out on the wide terrace (with tea and cakes in the afternoon) with its beguiling views up to the fairy-tale Moorish castle. And the garden is a delight; dripping with greenery, it has some old, old trees, a swimming pool lower down and a small play area for children. Multi-lingual Susana is a young, bright and caring hostess. The village centre with its numerous restaurants and shops is a short stroll away; for the more energetic, attractive paths lead steeply up to Sintra's castles and palaces.

rooms	10 doubles/twins.
price	€50–€85; single €45–€80.
meals	Snacks available all day. Good restaurants a 5-minute walk.
closed	Rarely.
directions	From Lisbon, IC19 for Cascais. Exit for Sintra & follow signs to S. Pedro. Hotel signed on right as you exit S.Pedro, towards historic centre of Sintra.

Susana Bezold Rosner Fragoso

tel	+351 219 230738
fax	+351 219 230738
e-mail	pensao.residencial.sintra@clix.pt

map 3　　entry 62

Casa Miradouro

Rua Sotto Mayor 55, PO Box 1027, 2710-801 Sintra, Lisboa

The gaily striped walls of Casa Miradouro make it an easy place to find as you wind down from Sintra. The present owner left a successful career in Switzerland to launch himself into restoring this light, elegant and airy home with views on all sides. Pass through a palm-graced porch, and a handsome bannistered staircase leads you up to the bedrooms. Here antique beds and wardrobes stand on sisal matting; ceilings are high and have the original stucco mouldings. It feels fresh and uncluttered, helped by the size of the rooms, the two in the attic included. Views are to the sea or to the hills. The sitting room has a similarly unfussy feel; here the sisal balances the flounced curtains. There is a bar with several different ports – and a hearth for sitting round in the colder months. Further downstairs is a modern breakfast room, simply decorated with four round tables and giving onto a large terrace. Classical music accompanies breakfast: cereals, cheeses, juices, yogurts, whatever fruit happens to be in season, savoury and sweet breads. Frederico is a gentle-mannered, attentive and truly charming host, his home as well-kept as any of Portugal's best.

rooms	6 doubles/twins.
price	€92-€122; singles €80-€109.
meals	Restaurants nearby.
closed	6 January-23 February. Check for 2004.
directions	From Lisbon, IC19 to Sintra. Follow brown signs for 'Centro Histórico'. At square by palace, right (in front of Hotel Central) & on to Tivoli Hotel. Down hill for 400m. House on left.

Frederico & Janda Kneubühl

tel	+351 219 235900
fax	+351 219 241836
e-mail	mail@casa-miradouro.com
web	www.casa-miradouro.com

Lawrence's Hotel

Rua Consigliéri Pedroso 38-40, Vila de Sintra, 2710-550 Sintra, Lisboa

Founded in 1764, it is the oldest hotel on the Iberian Peninsula. Everyone who was anyone wanted to stay here, and did – after Lord Byron's visit in 1809. He wouldn't recognise the modern "restaurant with rooms" that it has become today. "The guest comes first, last and is everything," is Dutchmann Jan Bos's philosophy and service is perfect without being ingratiating. (A waiter who worked here as a boy was absolutely delighted to return 40 years later, the day the hotel reopened!). Furnishings are elegant and comfortable yet refreshingly uncluttered. Bedrooms have wooden floors, firm beds, country-fresh fabrics and a romantic feel; bathrooms are top-notch, the best sporting hydro-massage baths. And then there's the restaurant. The menu is Portuguese rather than international, the food is impeccable and the wines the nation's best. Sintra is Portugal's pastry-capital and you will not be disappointed by your strawberry and raspberry *millefeuille* on its wild berry coulis. Breakfasts, too, are exquisite, whether croissants and pains au chocolat or English bacon and eggs. One of the most beguiling – and friendly – hotels we have come across, bang in Sintra's historic heart.

rooms	16: 11 doubles/twins; 5 suites.
price	€ 171–€ 235; single € 139–€ 182; suite € 299–€ 347.
meals	Dinner from € 40.
closed	Rarely.
directions	Hotel in Sintra city centre. Call for details on booking.

Jan Bos

tel	+351 219 105500
fax	+351 219 105505
e-mail	lawrences_hotel@iol.pt
web	www.portugalvirtual.pt/lawrences

map 3   entry 64

Quinta do Conde

Rua Quinta do Conde, Colares, 2710 Sintra, Lisboa

If you seek a house beautifully balanced in space, colour and comfort, book the 350 year-old Quinta do Conde, enfolded in the lush green coastal landscape at Colares. The approach is up a cobbled lane between creeper-strewn old houses; pass through an archway and you're in the peaceful flagstone courtyard, fragrant from orange and lemon trees. The Quinta, painted a creamy yellow, has been restored by Denise, a friendly, enthusiastic host whose taste and creativity are on display in the hand-painted touches, the sumptuous Pierre Frey and *toile de Jouy* fabrics, fine furniture and delightful colour combinations. Retire to a hand-painted four-poster or canopied bed: all are very, very comfortable, with rich covers and feather pillows. Marble bathrooms sport thick towels; breakfasts are served on Spode china. The salon is ballroom-size and has a patterned red-tile floor, orange and gold walls and an Italianate painted ceiling, all cherubs and flowers. Enjoy afternoon tea on the terrace with the old pecan tree and watch the sun go down. You can even see the sea from here: beaches are a five-minute drive.

rooms	8 doubles/twins.
price	€ 135–€ 180.
meals	Available locally.
closed	Occasionally.
directions	From Sintra San Pedro, take old road to Colares. Opp. church with coffee shop on left, left for Cascais Penedo. Up to top of hill & right down Rua da Quinta do Conde.

Denise O'Neill

tel	+ 44 (0)20 8332 9434
fax	+ 44 (0)20 8332 9434

Quinta Verde Sintra

Estrada de Magoito 84, Casal da Granja/Varzea de Sintra, 2710-252 Sintra, Lisboa

A modern house midway between Sintra and the beaches, Quinta Verde Sintra is set well back from the road, with distant green hills all around. This is a family home where Cesaltina, her husband Eugénio and sons Miguel and André create an easy, friendly atmosphere. Nature is bountiful here and the house is wrapped around by honeysuckle, bougainvillaea, palms, bay trees, cedar and succulents. Sitting rooms have comfortable sofas, terracotta floors and Portuguese flourishes, like the collection of old plates on the walls. The apartments have large sitting rooms and well-equipped kitchens, and the bedrooms have a mixture of wooden and metal beds, matching fabrics on drapes and bedspreads, and tiled floors softened with small rugs. Bathrooms sparkle. Breakfast, a generous spread, is taken at the tables-for-two in the breakfast room, with its large fireplace at one end, or, on summer mornings, out on the terrace, with views of the lush Sintra hills. See if you can pick out the Moorish castle, Pena Palace, Monserrate house, the Quinta da Regaleira and Palácio de Seteais.

rooms	5 doubles/twins. Self-catering apartments for 2-4.
price	€ 65-€ 90; single € 55-€ 80; apartments € 80-€ 150.
meals	Dinner by arrangement; light meals at any time.
closed	Rarely.
directions	From Sintra, signs to Ribeira de S.; to x-roads, pass tram lines to Café Miranda. After 1km, right for Magoito. After r'bout, left, then right. At Varzea, after 1.5km, on right.

Cesaltina de Sena

tel	+351 219 616069
fax	+351 219 608776
e-mail	mail@quintaverdesintra.com
web	www.quintaverdesintra.com

map 3   entry 66

Casa do Celeiro

Pé da Serra, Colares, 2705-255 Serra de Sintra, Lisboa

It's wild and inspiring up here in the Serra de Sintra, a lushly wooded National Heritage site. The farm buildings sit serenely on their hill with views of azure Atlantic waters and sunburnt fields; this really is a perfect place to unwind and to paint. Mary and Alan are friendly and relaxed. They teach small groups on 10-day painting holidays and exhibit their own work in Lisbon. They are also the architects responsible for the stylish renovation and extension of their 17th-century farmhouse. Upstairs is a two-story conservatory which can be used for painting; below is Alan's acrylic jewelery workshop. Above the house is a high pool built on an *eira* (stone threshing circle) with panoramic views. But it's not just the architecture that makes this place special, it's also the bohemian feel: sculptures in the courtyard, paintings in every corner, books on art and design, easels, brushes, dozens of plants and lots of quirky bits and pieces. Rooms are simply comfortable, with those views. Meals are communal with plenty of fresh Portuguese food, wine and conversation. And you don't have to paint to stay here – find your own space and relax: no pressure whatsoever. Heaven.

rooms	4: 3 doubles, 1 single.
price	€ 60; single € 45. Painting courses £600–£640 (full board & tuition).
meals	Dinner € 25, with wine.
closed	December–February.
directions	Lisbon-Cascaís; signs to Sintra via Azoia/Ulgueira on coast road to Pé da Serra. Approaching village, yellow wall on right next to steep road. Into village & turn back to go up same steep road to house.

Alan & Mary St George

tel	+351 219 280151
fax	+351 219 282480
e-mail	asgmsg@mail.telepac.pt
web	www.portugalpainting.com

Casal das Giestas

Rua do Alto da Bonita 112, Ranholas, 2710-185 Sintra, Lisboa

Plants with vibrant orange flowers climb all over this pretty cottage and there are plenty more in the walled garden too. A jasmine and wisteria-covered pergola overlooks the most fragrant setting for breakfast. Your hostess is a mine of information about Portuguese society and history and enjoys having guests to stay. Her house, built in the 1890s, has been redesigned and enlarged and has something of an English B&B feel: an old kitchen dresser in the dining room filled with English pottery, an oval dining table, silver candelabra, old prints and a beamed ceiling. Bedrooms are comfortable with good linen, wooden floors and rugs, dark antique furniture and plenty of books and English magazines. The gardens are quiet, calm and child-friendly with layered terraces, lush plants, magnolias and old trees; at night you may hear the hoot of an owl. Relax on the quiet lawn in the day; the chocolate, white and honey-coloured Labradors will keep you company. When you go out in the evening babysitting can be arranged: there's an abundance of romantic and interesting places to see and visit in Sintra, only a mile away. And it's a wonderfully short drive to those marvellous Atlantic beaches.

rooms	3 twins.
price	€ 90.
meals	Restaurants nearby.
closed	Rarely.
directions	From Lisbon, IC19 to Sintra, to Ranholas, then uphill. Right after large house with blue & white tiles. House on left.

Neilma Williams Egreja

tel	+351 219 234287
e-mail	casal.giestas@oninet.pt
web	www.casaldasgiestas.pt.vu/

map 3   entry 68

Fortaleza do Guincho

Relais & Châteaux, Estrada do Guincho, 2750-642 Cascais, Lisboa

The crest at this 17th-century cliff fortress reads 'Where the earth ends the sea begins'. As you are almost surrounded by the crashing Atlantic waves you tend to agree. This ochre-coloured oasis is metres from the most westerly point in Europe – walk to the other end of Guincho beach and you're there. There's an enormous, balconied, courtyard entrance with a high glass ceiling, suits of armour, modern chandeliers, leafy plants and tiled floors; follow the red carpet to the rooms upstairs. Bedrooms have watery views; in the suite you can watch or listen to the waves from bed – or close the double-glazed windows to the turbulent ocean. Bedrooms have archways, soft colourings, smart bedcovers, duckdown duvets, the heaviest curtains, the thickest bathrobes and every hotel luxury imaginable, from Nina Ricci soaps to treats on the pillows. The contrast between the hotel-style luxury everywhere inside the building and the wild windy turbulance on a blowy day outside is part of the fun. You can play at being rugged on that dramatic headland and then retreat for a slap-up dinner.

rooms	27: 24 doubles/twins, 3 suites.
price	€165–€330; single €155–€320; suite €285–€385.
meals	Lunch/dinner €38.
closed	Rarely.
directions	From Lisbon, A5 to Cascais, then EN91. At 1st r'bout follow signs for Birre; over 2nd r'bout following signs for Areia to Guincho Beach. Left at x-roads for 500m. Fortress on right, signed.

Isabel Ferreira Froufe

tel	+351 214 870491
fax	+351 214 870431
e-mail	reservations@guinchotel.pt
web	www.guinchotel.pt

Estalagem do Forte Muchaxo

Praia do Guincho, 2750 Cascais, Lisboa

Guincho is a long, curving sandy beach, backed by the Serra de Sintra – a perfect place from which to watch Atlantic sunsets. One of the best views is from Tony Muchaxo's inn, perched at one end of the beach. It's full of character, a fantastic combination of ocean liner and Neptune's grotto, with stone, cork pillars and strange wooden ceilings; floors are of *calçada*, parquet, slate, terracotta and marble, often sloping to adjust for the fact that it was all built on the ruin of an old fort. The restaurant has great views of the ocean, and the building is arranged around an inner courtyard where sea birds land among the succulents; there's plenty of peeling paint, too, but then the Guincho ocean is fierce. There are lots of plants inside, and, in the bar, a wishing well with running water, rock 'booths' and tree-trunk tabletops and pillars. Bedrooms are large and comfortable; pay the extra for the sea views. You feel you're almost in the brine, and you hear the raging waves all night – you have here an extraordinary mixture of wild nature, marble floors and beds with vinyl-padded bedheads. Eat in, or sample the many seafood restaurants along the coast and in cosmopolitan Cascais.

rooms	50 doubles/twins.
price	€45–€140.
meals	Dinner from €25.
closed	Rarely.
directions	In Cascais, follow signs to Guincho. Along coast wide beach as road turns inland. Forte Muchaxo on curve on left, a little below road.

António Muchaxo

tel	+351 214 870221
fax	+351 214 870444
e-mail	muchaxo@ip.pt
web	http://www.maisturismo.pt/emuchaxo

map 3   entry 70

As Janelas Verdes
Rua das Janelas Verdes 47, Javan Lda., 1200-690 Lisbon

In the old city, just yards from the Museum of Ancient Art, is this old, aristocratic townhouse – the great 18th-century novelist Eça de Queirós lived here. It is a perfect place to lay your head when in Lisbon. From the moment you are greeted by the smiling Palmira you feel like an honoured guest. To one side of the reception is the lounge, with marble-topped tables (you breakfast here in winter), a handsome fireplace, piano and comfortable chairs. In summer you can breakfast (or have a candlelit aperitif) on the patio. Enormous ficus and bougainvillaea run riot, a fountain gurgles and wrought-iron tables stand on dragon-tooth cobbling. A grand old spiral staircase leads you to the rooms, some of which have views of the river Tejo (book early if you want one). They are furnished with repro beds, flounced curtains and delicate pastel colours. Dressing gowns and towels are embroidered with the JV logo. And instead of a 'do not disturb' sign there's a hand-embroidered little pillow that says 'shhh!'. A delectable small hotel, that has been enlarged to include a library on the top floor with impressive views of that river.

rooms	29 doubles/twins.
price	€ 165–€ 195; luxury rooms € 198–€ 245.
meals	Breakfast € 12.50. Lunch & dinner available locally.
closed	Rarely.
directions	A2 m'way over River Tejo, then exit for Alcântara. Over r'bout; follow tram route for approx. 500m. Hotel on right, close to Muséo de Arte Antigo.

The Cardoso & Fernandes families

tel	+351 213 968143
fax	+351 213 968144
e-mail	jverdes@heritage.pt
web	www.heritage.pt

Pálacio Belmonte

Páteo Dom Fradique 14, 1100-624 Lisbon

A massively expensive, EU-subsidised restoration has brought the Palace into the 21st century with a bang; it was built for the Count Belmonte in the 15th century. Frederic is French, a specialist in sustainable development and won an award for urban regeneration for his use of natural and traditional materials: the traditional use of lime mortar gives walls a soft, warm feel. Each suite is as big as a house and all are elegant and understated, private and peaceful. The Bartolomeu de Gusmão suite is in the top of one of the Moorish towers and has an octagonal sitting room with a roof terrace, bedroom and bathroom, all on different levels up a spiral stone staircase. The Padre Himalaya suite is perfect for honeymooners, with circular views of Lisbon from the Roman tower. Bedrooms in warm colours have the softest sheets, heated terracotta tiles, antique furniture, original masonry; some have original frescoes, even and all have gorgeous bathrooms and phenomenal views. Luxurious simplicity at its simple best; each suite even has its owner designer aroma! The pool is heavenly — black marble with wooden decking, surrounded by orange and lemon trees.

rooms	8 suites.
price	€300-€900.
meals	Catering for groups only.
closed	Rarely.
directions	At the foot of Lisbon Castle, just outside walls. Call first to arrange a parking card.

Frederic Coustols

tel	+351 218 862582
fax	+351 218 862592
e-mail	office@palaciobelmonte.com
web	www.lagarde.org

map 3   entry 72

Solar do Castelo

Rua das Cozinhas, 2 (ao Castelo), Javan, Lda., 1100-181 Lisbon

The setting is spectacular – high up on the hill this new hotel sits within the pedestrian precinct of St Jorge's Castle overlooking the river Tejo and the centre of Lisbon. The building once housed the kitchens of the first Royal Palace – 800 years ago. It surrounds an inner courtyard and gardens and has ruins – such as the cistern – to explore. Décor is mainly modern with a beautiful mix of materials: marble, tiles, textiles, wood. Walk down corridors and see wooden floors, walls tiled in the Pombal star/flower/star pattern, wicker armchairs and chunky blue and grey pottery. Bedrooms are pristine, with marble bathrooms; large beds have wicker headboards. Some have exposed brick and timber walls, some stone and they all have rich textured fabrics, with linens, kilims and throws in natural colours: blues, terracottas, browns. The mansard bedrooms in the old part of the building have the best views. The courtyard garden is very pretty and you can breakfast here on wooden tables scattered in fresh flowers. There's a lovely tiled arch, water and patio pots – a haven in the city.

rooms	15: 4 doubles, 10 singles, 1 triple.
price	€ 165–€ 245; single € 155–€ 225; triple € 190–€ 315.
meals	Breakfast € 12.50. Lunch & dinner available locally.
closed	Rarely.
directions	Park in car park next to Lisboa Plaza & ask at reception for a taxi. Hotel in car-free precinct above city.

The Cardoso & Fernandes families

tel	+351 218 870909
fax	+351 218 870907
e-mail	solar.castelo@heritage.pt
web	www.heritage.pt

Residencial Alegria

Praça da Alegria 12, 1250-004 Lisbon

This family-run guest house could hardly be in a better position, yards from the street life of the Avenida de Liberdade yet in a quiet palm-fringed square which belies its inner-city status. It's all been freshly painted on the outside and you should approve of your room, too: "bright, cheerful, clean and basic" is how our inspector describes her favourite Lisbon digs. For the moment there is not much in the way of public space but Felix, the Alegria's likeable owner, has extended the ground floor into a larger breakfast room. Some rooms share bathrooms and a few are a shade drab with rather tired-looking bathrooms. Try to book our favourite room, number 114, which has been redecorated in a happy mix of blues and yellows (see photo). The double glazing is good for light sleepers; the corridors have been cleverly decorated in cheerful yellow and this and the shining parquet floors give the place a friendly atmosphere. An inexpensive and central address, close to restaurants and the capital's attractions – absolutely ideal for those on a tight budget.

rooms	41: 40 doubles/twins, 1 suite.
price	€28-€38; suite €38-€48.
meals	Restaurants nearby.
closed	Rarely.
directions	Turn off Avenida de Liberdade into Praça de Alegria. House between police station & 'bombeiros', behind Hotel Sofitel. Nearest metro: Avenida.

Felix Santos

tel	+351 213 220670
fax	+351 213 478070
e-mail	mail@alegrianet.com
web	www.alegrianet.com

map 3   entry 74

Residencial Florescente

Rua das Portas de Santo Antão 99, 1150 Lisbon

Another of the bright and cheerful family-run guest houses that we are happy to include alongside some rather grander neighbours. Over many years, Florescente has built up a reputation as a friendly, clean and fun stopover right at the heart of Pombaline Lisbon. You are brilliantly central yet spared the rumble of traffic; Santo Antão is a pedestrianised thoroughfare and a great place to sit out at a café or restaurant and watch the world go by. You dip in off the street into the small tiled reception area; a small fountain gurgles in the corner and the young staff are immediately attentive. The original bannistered and tiled staircase, more than a century old, leads up and up... and up. Narrowish corridors lead to the bedrooms which are mostly medium-sized and simply decorated with a very southern choice of print on the walls. There are high ceilings with stucco mouldings – a reminder of a more illustrious past. We loved the rather smaller attic rooms with their stand-up balconies, well worth the haul up to the fifth and top floor. No meals here, but just step outside and choose your café, restaurant or fruit shop. Ask for an air-conditioned room in the summer.

rooms	73: 64 doubles/twins, 9 suites.
price	€25–€50; suite €70–€80.
meals	Restaurants nearby.
closed	Rarely.
directions	In Lisbon, follow signs to centre; down Ave. de Liberdade. Park nr. Rossio in Restauradores car park. House approx. 100m north, in pedestrian street parallel to Liberdade. Metro: Restauradores.

Jacinta Antunes

tel	+351 213 425062
fax	+351 213 427733

Quinta de Santo Amaro

Aldeia da Piedade, 2925-375 Azeitão, Lisboa

Looking out to the Arrábida mountains, this genteel *quinta* was where the de Mello family would pass the summer months. Maria had fond memories of it all from her childhood and later decided to make it her first home and bring new life by opening her doors to guests. We loved the bedrooms and apartment because of their deliciously homely feel; each one is very individual, too. For children there is an attic with five beds. There are planked floors and ceilings in what is called 'the middle house', and attractive wooden beds. In the apartment are oil paintings and hearths, part-period bathrooms and a piano. When you arrive, it is to a bottle of wine and, in winter, to a log fire in the apartment. It is a wonderful base for several nights, for Lisbon is an easy drive, as are the beaches of the Setúbal peninsula, and the local Fonseca wine cellars are well worth visiting. Breakfast is a help-yourself feast of home-made breads, jams, cheeses, ham and freshly-squeezed orange juice from Amaro's groves. But what makes it all so very special is Maria herself, a lady with boundless enthusiasm and energy; heed her advice on where to eat and what to visit. *Minimum three nights.*

rooms	2 doubles; 1 self-catering apt for 6.
price	€ 80; apt € 220 (€ 1,280 per week).
meals	Good restaurants nearby.
closed	Rarely.
directions	From Lisbon, m'way for Setúbal. Exit for Azeitão, then Sesimbra; route 378 to r'bout at Santana; left to Azeitão on route 379 for 6km. At Café Estrela dos Arcos, left for Estrada dos Arcos. House at end.

Maria da Pureza O'Neill de Mello
tel +351 212 189230
fax +351 212 189390

map 5 entry 76

Solar de Alvega

EN 118-km149, Alvega, 2205-104 Abrantes, Santarém

The Marquês de Pombal built it in the 18th century and it is as imposing as ever, with views to the stream, tall walnut trees a waterfall and countryside beyond. Maria Luiza and her English husband Paul met in Africa and bought the house in 1998. Since then they have restored it to its former grandeur and introduced interesting juxtapositions of English and Portuguese antiques: Staffordshire figures cheek-by-jowl with blue and white *faience*, an English grandfather clock ticking to an old Portuguese flag. Maria has restored many of the antiques and other *objets* herself, from antique letter-scales to Art Nouveau lamps and intricate furniture. Sumptuous bedrooms have polished parquet floors and antique beds with elaborate wooden headboards; all are different – one room in the tower has five windows and access to the *mirante*, the roofed balcony; another opens onto a beautiful little chapel. They may do weddings here soon and the bridal suite has the only original bathroom: cool pink and black marble. And do try the *jardineira* stew: mixes meat and vegetables with potatoes and peas – delicious.

rooms	6 doubles/twins/family rooms.
price	€70–€80; single €60; family rooms from €85.
meals	Lunch €15; dinner €20, booked the previous day.
closed	February.
directions	A1 Lisbon-Oporto. Exit Torres Novas; east on IP6; exit Mouriscas. Signs for Castelo Branco & Portalegre. House 5km after exit from IP6.

Paul Mallett

tel	+351 917 610579
fax	+351 213 161114
e-mail	solaralvega@yahoo.co.uk
web	www.solardealvega.com

Quinta do Troviscal

Alverangel - Castelo de Bode, 2300 Tomar, Santarém

If you love water, you'll love Troviscal. The house, which looks out across the vast reservoir at Castelo de Bode, offers peace, boating, swimming and long walks. Vera, ex-history teacher, and João, a surveyor, are an engaging couple with three children and their home is a modern, long-fronted villa at the edge of an inlet surrounded by tall pines, poplars and eucalyptus. The colours are the traditional yellow and white, the proportions are good, and the décor a smooth blend of modern and traditional Portuguese. There is excellent use of natural materials: American oak ceilings, slate floors, hand-painted St Anna bathroom tiles. Beds are comfortable and all rooms open onto a long shaded terrace where breakfasts are served. After your feast of home-made cake, fruit, yogurt, coffee, tea you can stroll down the terraces and through shaded pergolas — one a tunnel of wisteria, bliss in the spring — to the Troviscal's floating pontoon. All around is water and forest; you may see an eagle soaring above. Castelo de Bode is a wonderful place, and the water is warm for much of the year. "Perfection", said our inspector.

rooms	3: 2 doubles, 1 suite.
price	€ 70-€ 75; suite €85-€ 110.
meals	Available locally.
closed	Rarely.
directions	From Tomar or Lisbon follow signs to Castelo de Bode. Straight on for 6km & follow signs for Quinta do Troviscal & Turismo Rural; after 2km sign points to a track to right. Follow track to Quinta.

Vera Sofia Sepulveda de Castel Branco

tel	+351 249 371318
fax	+351 249 371862
e-mail	vera@troviscal.com
web	www.troviscal.com

map 3   entry 78

Casa dos Monstros

Alverangel - Castelo de Bode, 2300 Tomar, Santarém

Just the other side of the track from the Quinta (see entry 78) is a little stone house impeccably restored – Vera's self-catering *casa*. Gleaming terracotta floors, white walls, pine ceilings, soft lights – a rather special home-from-home. The single-storey house has a cheery lounge with built-in seating and a sofabed (handy for teenagers); then a well-equipped kitchen/diner where three French windows lead to a large, beautifully cobbled terrace, with furniture, pergola and barbecue. There's no washing machine, but bed linen and towels are regularly changed. One of the two double bedrooms has bunk beds tucked away around the corner – four adults and two children would be very comfortable here. A scamper down the stepped bank brings you to the lake with private pontoon, an idyllic spot for sun-lovers. Swim in the turquoise waters, bask on the sunlounger, slip off in the row boat to the opposite shore. Should you require shade, there are the family's neat lawns and lovely garden to retreat to. You are 10 minutes from the shops, 15 minutes from restauants; Vera, ever helpful and friendly, will present you with her own little eating out guide. *Minimum three day stay.*

rooms	Self-catering house for 4-8.
price	€ 150–€ 175.
meals	Restaurants nearby.
closed	Rarely.
directions	From Tomar or Lisbon follow signs to Castelo de Bode. Straight on for 6km & follow signs for Quinta do Troviscal & Turismo Rural; after 2km sign points to a track to right. Follow track to Quinta.

Vera Sofia Sepulveda de Castel Branco

tel	+351 249 371318
fax	+351 249 371862
e-mail	vera@troviscal.com
web	www.troviscal.com

Casa da Avó Genoveva

Rua 25 de Abril 16, Curvaceiras, 2305-509 Tomar, Santarém

You are just outside beautiful Tomar and its Templar castle, but what first impresses you on arrival at Avó Genoveva is the serenity of the place. The huge old palm trees and pots of geraniums in the dragon-tooth courtyard, combined with the soft salmon and white of the buildings, lend a southern charm. José or Manuela usher you through to public rooms which are plush but homely; in the lounge there are family photos, woodburner, piano and card table while in the dining room are antique dressers and a collection of old crockery – not a bit hotelly. You're spoiled for choice when deciding where to settle: in the music room feel free to put on a record (classical and *fado* in abundance), the snooker room doubles as a library and there is a small bar, well stocked with Portuguese wines. And what bedrooms! Dark pine ceilings, family antiques, old paintings; doubles are up an old stone staircase in the main house, while the apartments are across the way in the old granary. Not far from the house are tennis court, swings and pool – and there are bikes, too. Your hosts are kindly, educated people who delight in sharing their wonderful home.

rooms	6 doubles; 2 apartments.
price	€ 70; apartment for 2 € 90, for 4 € 130.
meals	Available locally.
closed	Rarely.
directions	From Tomar towards Lisbon. After 9km, in Guerreira, right to Curvaceiras. After 4km, house signed on left.

José & Manuela Gomes da Costa

tel	+351 249 982219
fax	+351 249 981235

map 3   entry 80

Quinta da Alcaidaria - Mór

2490 Ourém, Santarém

This lovely wisteria-clad manor has been the family seat for more than 300 years and is every inch the grand country house: stately cedar-lined main drive, box-hedged gardens and its own private chapel. The main house is a cool, gracious building – light streams in to the high-ceilinged rooms while marble floors, arches and delicate plaster work remind you that you are in the south. Don't miss the chance to dine (inexpensively) around the enormous *pau santo* dining table. The chandeliers and collection of old china may inspire you to dress for dinner. Guest apartments are in a converted outbuilding; doubles are in the main house and most pukka they are too. There are old dressers, Dona Maria beds, comfortable chairs, perhaps a grand old tub with clawed feet; all rooms have beautiful moulded pine ceilings and big bathrooms and are generously tiled and marbled. Each is different from the next; all are first-class. Add to this the natural kindness of your English-speaking hosts (they often invite guests to join them for a glass of fine port) and you begin to get the measure of this charming guest house. *Minimum stay three nights.*

rooms	6 doubles/twins; 2 apts for 4-6.
price	€90–€115; apts €115–€125.
meals	Light snacks; dinner, €17.50, on request.
closed	Rarely.
directions	From Ourém, towards Tomar. After 2km, road curves right, left at sign 'Turismo de Habitação'.

The Vasconcelos Family

tel	+351 249 542231
fax	+351 249 545034
e-mail	geral@quintaalcaidaria-mor.pt
web	www.quintaalcaidaria-mor.pt

Casa do Patriarca

Rua Patriarca D. José 134, Atalaia, 2260-039 Vila Nova da Barquinha, Santarém

This 500-year-old house has been the home of the d'Oliveira family for five generations. You may be greeted by Manuel's son, his daughter or his wife, as well as by two friendly boxers. The lounge has French windows leading to the walled garden. It is a long, low room, comfortable rather than grand, and a cool retreat in summer months. Just off it is a small kitchen for guests, a thoughtful touch for families not wanting to eat out. The long breakfast table is beautifully laid with home-made fruit and delicacies, and you can also have the full English version; in winter your juice will be fresh from Manuel's oranges. Bedrooms are delightful, each decorated to a different theme. Quinta has the great-great-grandfather's bed; Oriente has lamps and cushions from India, Almirante a naval theme and Sana Sana evokes Mozambique where your hosts spent their honeymoon. Outside, the huge gardens are a real pleasure. An enormous date palm towers above the pomegranate, medlar, orange and fig trees, there are shady spots in which to sit and relax, and a pool edged by trees. Manuel and his family are very caring and staying here is a treat.

rooms	6 doubles.
price	€50-€75.
meals	Self-catering option.
closed	Rarely.
directions	From m'way, exit 1 for Torres Novas, then IP6, then IC3 for Tomar. After 1500m signed for Atalaia & house.

Manuel d'Oliveira

tel	+351 249 710581
fax	+351 249 711191
e-mail	mop59265@mail.telepac.pt
web	casadopatriarca.pt.vu

map 3   entry 82

Casa da Reserva de Burros

Estrada das Grutas, Porto de Mos, 2480-034 Alvados , Santarém

Gentle, friendly Paolo set up this unusual donkey sanctuary many years ago; he now breeds them, too. He adores these gentle creatures and will take you on day-trips into the mountains. The rustic self-catering apartments are in a large granite cottage in the middle of the rugged hills. Bedrooms are simple with wide views, colourful bedspreads, freshly painted walls and carved wooden bedsteads. Paolo has added special touches – a stone trough sink here, a porcelain bowl on a pretty washstand there – which give a contemporary slant to the décor. You can watch local weavers making beautiful stripey rugs and bedcovers and buy wild herbs and honey. The cavernous restaurant – sometimes used by coach visitors who come for the day to experience this wonderful place – has a central free-standing oven and hay-bale seating which fits perfectly. Paolo knows the surrounding National Park area like the back of his hand and is always happy to advise on things to do and see. Visit the nearby caves, walk in the spectacular mountains, hire a bike nearby or just revel in the serenity of the landscape. Poppies grow everywhere and the sunsets are inspiring.

rooms	3 self-catering apartments for 2-4.
price	€ 110-€ 196, for 2.
meals	Restaurant and snack bar.
closed	Rarely.
directions	Leave A1 at exit 7 (Torres Novas) & follow signs for Grutas/Serra de Santo António. In Moitas Venda, left & keep following same signs.

Paolo Arojo

tel	+351 249 841034
fax	+351 249 841166
e-mail	reserva-de-burros@mail.telepac.pt
web	www.reserva-de-burros.pt

Quinta do Vale de Lobos

Azoia de Baixo, 2000-443 Santarém, Santarém

Such is the veiled privacy of this old manor house that the Portuguese saying 'to go to the Vale de Lobos' came to mean to go back to nature, to escape from the madding crowd. Nowadays, from the lush gardens, through the trees, you may just hear traffic in the distance but staying here remains a deeply restful experience. Veronica and Joaquim share their large home with their four children, their housekeeper Cidalia and their guests. This much-travelled, polyglot couple receive you with great charm and their home is the sort in which most of us would love to live. Nothing superfluous or showy: elegant simplicity is the key note. The sitting room is light and cheery with striped curtains, deep sofas and an attractive wood and terracotta floor. There are books and magazines galore, many about things equestrian — you are in the Ribatejo, after all. We liked the bedrooms where the ornately turned Bilros beds, high ceilings, balconies and pretty bathrooms mirror the mood of the public rooms. The apartments are a treat, too; rather more modern in style, they have cleverly hidden kitchenettes and would be ideal for a longer stay

rooms	4 doubles/twins; 2 self-catering apartments.
price	€80. Apartment for 4 €95.
meals	Lunch and snacks available.
closed	23-31 December.
directions	From Santarém, N3 for Torres Novas. Through Portela das Padeiras; just past turning for Azoia de Baixo, over small bridge. Road turns left & climbs. As it bends right, left into drive.

Veronica & Joaquim Santos Lima

tel	+351 243 429264
fax	+351 243 429313
e-mail	valedelobos@mail.telepac.pt
web	www.valedelobos.com

map 3   entry 84

Quinta da Cortiçada

Outeiro da Cortiçada, 2040 Rio Maior, Santarém

Few settings are as utterly peaceful as that of Quinta da Cortiçada; this soft-salmon-coloured building, reached by a long poplar-lined avenue, sits in the greenest of valleys. As we arrived a heron rose from the lake and flapped slowly away, a graceful welcome – so too was the gentle smile of the housekeeper who was waiting at the main entrance. Inside the building the silence feels almost monastic – birdsong instead of vespers. You have the choice of two lounges; one has a games table and high French windows on two sides, and is dignified by the family *oratorio* (altarpiece). The other leads to a covered veranda with wicker tables and chairs. Cortiçada feels most homelike in the dining room where, if you dine in, you'll rub shoulders with your fellow guests round the old oval table. Along the marble corridor the rooms have old Dona Maria beds, antique dressers, thick rugs on pine floors… all of it is utterly pristine. Bathrooms are four-star plush, while sensitive lighting and carefully chosen fabrics help to make it extra special. And, like that heron, you're welcome to fish in the lake.

rooms	6 doubles/twins, 2 suites.
price	€88-€113; suite €106-131; single €76-100.
meals	Lunch/dinner €21, by arrangement.
closed	Christmas Day.
directions	From Lisbon A1 north for Porto. Exit at Santarém on EN114 for Rio Maior. In Secorio, Quinta signed on right. After 12km (2km after Outeiro), pink farm in valley.

Teresa Nobre

tel	+351 243 470000
fax	+351 243 470009
e-mail	quinta.corticada@mail.telepac.pt
web	www.quintacorticada.com

Casa do Foral

Rua da Boavista 10, 2040 Rio Maior, Santarém

This 19th-century townhouse is both pretty and unusual. Outside it is attractive with an ivy-clad front, pebble cobbles and cast-iron porch. Inside is unusual: the owner's love of collecting has turned the place into something of a museum, with collections of one sort or another at every turn – penknives, bottle-openers, tankards, plates, fox-hunting prints, even walking sticks. There's a pleasantly quiet atmosphere here and you are looked after by the friendly housekeeper Margarida. The large, old-style lounge has plenty of sofas – as well as collections of brass and copper and old guns – and the dining room has a rustic wooden table, leather chairs, beams and an old *azulejo* frieze. The breakfast room is modern and minimalist in comparison, almost café-like with its wicker chairs, glass tables and glass wall looking onto an interior courtyard and lovely pepper tree. Outside are palms, oleander, a rose pergola for shade and a pool next to the beautifully designed modern section. Bedrooms are comfortable and light with pine bedheads and shutters and lots of pale green; one has a glass wall, another a wooden mezzanine. A unique house of much character, a shortish walk from the village.

rooms	6 doubles/twins.
price	€65; single €48.
meals	Restaurants nearby.
closed	Rarely.
directions	From A1 Lisbon-Porto or from A15 Santarem-Caldas da Rainha; exit Rio Main. In Rio Maior, house signed.

Carlos Higgs Madeira

tel	+351 243 992610
fax	+351 243 992611
e-mail	moinhoforal@hotmail.com

map 3   entry 86

Quinta da Ferraria

Ribeira de S. João, 2040 Rio Maior, Santarém

Quinta da Ferraria stands amid vineyards and olive groves; a channel cut from the nearby river powered the mill and ran a turbine powerful enough to light up the whole farm in the days before electricity arrived. Recently the farm was totally renovated to create a handsome small country hotel; it has been set up for both business and pleasure, and the exceptionally green and peaceful setting and the abundance of water make it special enough to please both types of guest. Bedrooms have new pine floors and ceilings, soft Alcobaça fabrics and bathrooms with head-to-toe tiling. Pine is also the main feature of the sitting room; sisal matting, rugs and an open hearth add warmth to a very large space. The dining room, by contrast, feels somewhat soulless due to its wedding-banquet dimensions. But this is a good stopover, especially for a family, with the riding stables and farm museum. Next to the dining room you can still see the original olive-milling machinery. And, as the brochure points out, here are "blue-distanced horizons and clear, sparkling air to invigorate, stimulate and enhance life and living"!

rooms	13: 12 doubles/twins, 1 suite; 2 self-catering apartments.
price	€82–€98; suite €89–€115; single €70–€83; apt €121–€146.
meals	Lunch/dinner €21, by arrangement.
closed	24-25 December.
directions	From Lisbon, A1 north for Porto. Exit at Santarém on EN114 for Rio Maior. After Ribeira di S. João, Signed on left on your left; up track next to football pitch to house.

Teresa Nobre

tel	+351 243 945001
fax	+351 243 945696
e-mail	quinta.ferraria@mail.telepac.pt
web	www.quintaferraria.com

Finca El Cabezo

San Martín de Trevejo, 10892 Cáceres, Spain

It is an awe-inspiring journey across the western reaches of the province of Cáceres to the farm: rolling hills, cork oak forests, kites and eagles overhead... and the road virtually to yourself. You are headed for a working farm of more than 1,000 olive trees and a hundred head of cattle but don't expect to cross a muddy farmyard. Pass through the gates of this imposing granite-built farm and you enter a magical inner courtyard, softened by a rambling Virginia creeper and a mass of potted plants. The guest rooms are in the eastern wing and their size and elegance come as a surprise: the decoration mixes old granite and antiques with parquet, warm paint schemes and modern art. The sitting room, too, would have the designer-mag people purring: slate floors and granite walls juxtapose warm paintings and fabrics. Feast on eggs fried in olive oil, goat's cheese and home-made cakes at breakfast, and at dinner, choose between cheerful restaurants in San Martín or a Michelin-listed eatery just down the road. And find time to go for a walk. Finca El Cabezo may be in one of Spain's furthest flung corners but it is worth the detour.

rooms	6: 5 doubles/twins, 1 suite.
price	€ 76; suite € 89.
meals	Restaurants nearby.
closed	Rarely.
directions	From Salamanca for Ciudad Rodrigo. Here towards Cáceres & once you are over the pass of 'Puerto de los Perales' right for Valverde del Fresno on Ex-205. House on left at km22.8 post, signed.

Miguel, Muriel & María Moreno

tel	+34 927 193106
fax	+34 927 193106
e-mail	correo@elcabezo.com
web	www.elcabezo.com

Photography courtesy of Quinta do Barranco da Estrada, entry no 121

SOUTHERN PORTUGAL

"The village of Sintra is... the most delightful in Europe: it contains beauty of every description natural and artificial"

LORD BYRON

Quinta da Bela Vista
7320-014 Póvoa e Meadas, Portalegre

The gently undulating hills planted with cork and olive, the long vistas and sense of space of this part of Portugal make a visit here more than just a holiday... you are touched on a deeper level. The Quinta da Bela Vista is at the edge of a tiny Alentejo village, and Dona Maria's family have been here since the 1920s, when an uncle built the nearby dam. This is a family home, where books, magazines, photos, piano and card-table create a mood of intimacy while vast reception rooms, chandeliers and maid evoke one of privilege. Of the bedrooms we liked Rosa best – no numbers here, insists Maria – which is decorated in a white-on-pink print of flying ducks and has a veranda with a view and a period bathroom. All bedrooms are large, have wooden floors and are really quiet; most have views out to nearby Castelo de Vide. Rather like staying with a favourite aunt, you enjoy family recipes (much of the meat is from the farm) and the Quinta's own wine and *aguardente* (grape liqueur) and fresh eggs. A good place for a family stay: food and drink are always available and children will enjoy the huge games room, while outside there are a pool, tennis court, bicycles and horses.

rooms	4 doubles/twins; 2 self-catering houses.
price	€75; single €63. Houses for 1-6 €120-€165.
meals	Lunch/dinner €15.
closed	5-20 January.
directions	From Lisbon, A1 to Torres Novas, then IP6 to Saida. From Saida IP2, then N118 for Nisa & on to Póvoa e Meadas. House signed.

Maria Teresa Monteiro dos Santos
tel   +351 245 968125
fax   +351 245 968132
e-mail   belavista@mail.pt

map 4   entry 89

Casa do Parque

Avenida da Aramenha 37, 7320 Castelo de Vide, Portalegre

In a beautiful backwater of the Alentejo, surrounded by stands of chestnut and acacia, the hilltop village of Castelo de Vide is girt around with its 13th-century town wall. Steep cobblestone alleys run up the hill through the old Jewish *call* to the castle; make sure to visit the spring whose waters are said to cure everything. The focal point of the lower town is the leafy Praça Dom Pedro V and tucked away at one end of it you will find the gaily canopied Casa do Parque. The family are proud of their *hospitalidade portuguesa*; the feeling of homeliness spills over into the prettily furnished guest bedrooms. They are surprisingly well furnished (even though bathrooms are smallish) and are spotlessly clean; they have attractive wooden furniture and mattresses that lead you gently into the arms of Morpheus. In winter, hot-air heating warms the room in minutes. Don't miss dinner in the restaurant downstairs and the *migas alentejanas*, or one of the roast dishes; the dining room is a large, functional affair where you may be the only foreigner among local diners. Guests can enjoy a pool a kilometre away, at the owners' Casa dos Lilazes, which also has 10 rooms. *Private swimming pool 1km*

rooms	25 doubles/twins, 1 suite.
price	€ 45–€ 55; single € 30–€ 40; suite € 58–€ 65.
meals	Lunch/dinner € 14.
closed	Rarely.
directions	From Portalegre, E802 for Marvão, then left on E246 to Castelo de Vide. Into centre, then right along top of park; hotel at end on left.

Victor Guimarães

tel	+351 245 901250
fax	+351 245 901228

Albergaria El Rei Dom Miguel

Rua Bartolomeu Alvares da Santa 45, 7320 Castelo de Vide, Portalegre

Castelo de Vide is one of the Alentejo's most memorable hilltop villages; within the town walls built by Dom Afonso in the 13th century, the old Jewish quarter (you can visit the synagogue) climbs anarchically up towards the castle. Just to one side of the lower town's main square is this fine old townhouse, a small B&B. A granite staircase leads to the first floor and the living quarters but the house's most salient feature is its polished wooden flooring. The many antiques in the lounge and corridors give away Dona Maria Ribeiro's passion for period furniture. We particularly liked the quiet drawing room with its old oratorio and figure of São Domingo and open hearth (there is always a fire in the colder months). Bedrooms, each with private bathroom, are more contemporary in feel; wooden beds, writing and bedside tables are new, as are curtains and bedspreads in matching (local) fabric. Special wall insulation and double glazing guarantee a warm, peaceful night and the whole of the house is spic and span. Excellent value at any time of the year and there's a cheerful little restaurant just yards away.

rooms	7 twins.
price	€ 40–€ 60.
meals	Restaurants nearby.
closed	Rarely.
directions	From Portalegre, E802 for Marvão, then left on E246 to Castelo de Vide. At main square of town, left into main street (Carreira de Cima). Hotel on left.

Maria Vitoria Ribeiro Chamiço Heitor

tel	+351 245 919191
fax	+351 245 901592

map 4   entry 91

Pomar Velho

Galegos, 7330-072 Marvão, Portalegre

On the Spanish frontier, an 18th-century stone farmhouse set in five acres of terraced land dotted with fruit, olive and cork oak trees. A huge mulberry shades the front of the house and the terrace – a perfect spot for an aperitif. From the pool muse at the spectacular Sao Marmede mountain range; if the mood takes you, explore the surrounding hills. The high-ceilinged lounge has wooden beams, terracotta floors and plump sofas (and, usefully, lots of games). Sweep down Art Deco stairs to the dining room where the stone bread oven has been turned into a fireplace. Beams are the original chestnut, and the granite grape press is as old as the house. Bedrooms are fresh and crisp: blue-wash furniture, white walls, white bedspreads and local pottery; bathroom sparkle. Marvão Castle dominates this mountain village where festivals take place throughout the year; the Chestnut Festival is particularly special – people open their houses to artisans, the council subsidises the wine and the party begins! Carole and Ken are English, kind and welcoming and cook wonderful Portuguese and English food; dinners are four-course feasts. *Uninspected at time of going to press.*

rooms	4 doubles/twins.
price	€ 60–€ 75.
meals	Lunch € 8; dinner € 30.
closed	22 December–2 January.
directions	From main road to Spain, left at sign to Galegos. Pass through village, then, as road starts to descend, take 1st track on right for 200m. Park at end of track & ring bell at gate.

Ken & Carole Parr

tel	+351 245 964465
e-mail	parryoung@pomarv.jazznet.pt
web	www.pomarv.jazznet.pt

Tapada do Barreiro

Carreiras, Castelo de Vide, 7300 Portalegre

The charming farmhouse sits 500m above the village of Carreiras, in the heart of the São Mamede Natural Park. The whole area is beautiful with wooded hills, rocky crests and fertile valleys running along the Spanish frontier. Sensitively modernized, this is an excellent holiday home: fresh white walls, modern terracotta floors, wooden ceilings wonderfully rustic. The ground floor is given over almost entirely to the kitchen/dining room; French windows open onto a terrace with views over the Alentejo – a heavenly spot for sunset-watching. The bathroom, with washing machine, is also on this floor. Upstairs are three good-sized, wooden-floored bedrooms, two with great views, and a sitting room with log-burner. The garden – with a tiny dip pool – leads into open hillside studded with olive groves and cork trees. Everything you could wish for is here: a shop, bar and restaurant in the village below, the hill-top village of Marvão for good eating out, the Apartadura lake for swimming and fishing, a fine golf course and great walks. Peter, the English owner who lives nearby, can take you on birdwatching and walking trips.

rooms	Self-catering farmhouse.
price	€ 400–€ 500 (2 adults) per week; extra adult € 100, child (2-12) € 50.
meals	Restaurant nearby.
closed	Rarely.
directions	House up in the hills, 8km from Portalegre & 6km from Castelo de Vide. Call owner on booking for directions.

Peter & Rosemary Eden

tel	+351 268 629899
fax	+351 268 629899
e-mail	peter_eden@hotmail.com

map 4   entry 93

Casa de Borba

Rua da Cruz 5, 7150-125 Borba, Évora

A gem of a house, it was built by Madame's family at the end of the 17th century; the surrounding estate is given over to olives, vineyards and livestock. The building earns a mention in the *inventário artístico de Portugal*; once you pass through the main entrance, an extraordinary neo-classical staircase leads you to the first-floor living quarters. (Ask for help with heavy bags: there is no lift.) Fine bedrooms have high, delicately moulded ceilings, parquet floors softened by Arraiolos rugs, and are crammed with the family antiques. The Bishop's Room (where the Archbishop of Évora stayed) has an 18th-century canopied bed; Grandmother's Room has an unusual lift-up sink. There are baths with feet, old prints, and long curtains in front of the windows looking over a delectable garden. The lounge and breakfast room are similarly elegant; breakfast arrives via the 'dumb waiter'. Your hosts are quiet, refined folk and they skimp on nothing to please you; at night, hot water is delivered to your room together with cake and a selection of teas. During the day choose between the long covered gallery, a corner of the walled garden or the billiard room. A house of beauty and tranquillity.

rooms	5 doubles/twins.
price	€80; single €70.
meals	Restaurants nearby.
closed	20-28 December.
directions	From Estremoz, N4 to Borba. House in town centre, close to post office (Correios).

Maria José Tavares Lobo de Vasconcellos
tel   +351 268 894528
fax   +351 268 841448

Hotel Convento de São Paulo

Aldeia da Serra, 7170-120 Redondo, Évora

Superb in all respects, this massive monastery was built by Paulist monks who came to the D'Ossa mountain slopes in the 12th century. For 500 years they embellished their place of worship and imbued it with an atmosphere of deep spirituality and calm: as you pass through the enormous old door your voice instinctively drops. The 54,000 hand-painted tiles that decorate chapel, corridors and gardens are the largest collection in Europe. A red carpet softens the terracotta floors and sweeps you along to the rooms. Each occupies two cells, the uncluttered feel in keeping with São Paulo's past, though the bathrooms have brass taps and white marble. The 'public' rooms are no less interesting, for there are some lovely pieces, many of them heirlooms of the Leotte family. The great vaulted ceilings avoid overwhelming the cosy dining room and the sitting room; eclectic modern art lends a lighter note, and there are cloisters and a games room, too. Outside, enjoy the beautiful tiled patio depicting the four seasons, a swimming pool shaded by trees, views and walks through the wooded slopes of the 600-hectare estate which provides fruit, vegetables and meat. The spirit soars.

rooms	33 doubles/twins.
price	€ 180–€ 195; single € 145–€ 167.
meals	Lunch/dinner € 60.
closed	Rarely.
directions	From Lisbon on m'way for Madrid. Exit for Estremoz, then towards Elvas for approx. 5km, then for Redondo. Hotel 15km further.

Porfírio Perdigão

tel	+351 266 989160
fax	+351 266 989167
e-mail	hotelconvspaulo@mail.telepac.pt
web	www.hotelconventospaulo.com

map 4   entry 95

Casa de Peixinhos

7160 Vila Viçosa, Évora

Casa de Peixinhos is, like vintage port, a rich, mellow experience, the fruit of time and patience. Once you pass under the main portal and into the cobbled courtyard, the main façade has a distinctly exotic feel; its arches and triple turrets are softened by whitewashed walls with broad bands of ochre. Inside the main building the mood is more classical; this is a superbly maintained aristocratic house and, though much of the décor and furnishing is period, everything sparkles freshly. The sitting room is a handsome introduction to the house, with mouldings, a leather three-piece and the family coat of arms above the hearth. Leading off it is the dining room, with mouldings enhanced by gold drapes, chandeliers and beautifully arranged flowers. This is the sort of place where you might dress for the traditional Alentejo dinner. Rooms are among the loveliest we have come across in Portugal, some decorated in blues, others in *sang de boeuf*, and each one different. One has Dona Maria beds, another canopied twins; all of them have gorgeous bathrooms with local marble. A regal house.

rooms	8: 7 doubles/twins, 1 suite.
price	€98; single €78; suite €130.
meals	Lunch/dinner €20.
closed	Rarely.
directions	From Évora to Vila Viçosa. There, follow signs for Borba into Vila V. town centre. Just past Mercado Municipal, left & follow signs.

José Passanha

tel	+351 268 980472
fax	+351 268 881348

Herdade do Monte Branco

Rio de Moinhos, 7150 BRB Borba, Évora

Few places can be more tranquil than this estate on the sunny flanks of a hillside near Borba. The Herdade is well off the beaten track, a restored farmhouse and outbuildings that have been converted into apartments by one of the owners, architect José Calado, and sleeping between two and eight. They are very well furnished in Alentejo style, with old furniture, much of it hand-painted in the local floral style. The tiles in the bathrooms and kitchens have been painted by José's wife, artist Maria João, and the bedrooms are countrified and simple, with whitewashed walls, exposed beams, tiled floors and comfortable beds. You wake to the sounds of birds and rustling trees. There's a pool, a large, rustic games room/bar and a dining room where the food is good – you need never cook in, and breakfast is included in the price. The Herdade is near cork trees and forest and a lovely short walk to a freshwater lake hidden in the trees. Your hosts are friendly, educated people who readily share their enthusiasm for this region. Other diversions may include visits to the centres of cork, wine and cheese production; you can also go clay-pigeon shooting and visit prehistoric sites. An ideal spot for nature-lovers and families.

rooms	9 self-catering apartments for 2-8.
price	€55–€90 per room. Weekly rates available.
meals	Lunch €35; dinner €38.
closed	Rarely.
directions	On A2 from Lisbon, southbound, A6 eastbound; exit at Estremoz & join N4. Follow signs to Gloria & then to Rio de Moinhos. Monte Branco signed to right.

The Medeiros family

tel	+351 214 830834
fax	+351 214 863403
e-mail	montebranco@netcabo.pt
web	pwp.netcabo.pt/0218645001

map 4   entry 97

Casa de Terena

Rua Direita 45, 7250-065 Terena-Alandroal, Évora

If you approach Terena from the north, all you see is the medieval castle. The village, still pretty unspoilt, has developed on the hill's south-western slopes in typical whitewashed Alentejo style. Groups of village ladies were sunning themselves, bent over their lace, the day that we visited and we could see why Conchita and António were inspired to move here from Lisbon. It was a labour of love to nurse this grand old 18th-century village house back to life. From the inner dragon-tooth patio a grand marble staircase sweeps you up to the bedrooms. Here you'll find wrought-iron bedsteads (with new mattresses), Alentejo rugs, terracotta tiles, dried flowers, private bathrooms and views out to the reservoir beyond. Casablanca-style ceiling fans cool things down when the heat sets in. The downstairs sitting room has wafer-bricked, vaulted ceilings, a large fireplace, red and blue armchairs and dark red velvet curtains; it's a good room for *tertulias*, late-night conversations. The tranquillity and beauty of Terena and your hosts' enthusiasm make the journey worthwhile. Ornithologists – bring your binoculars.

rooms	6 doubles/twins.
price	€ 70; single € 60; extra bed € 30.
meals	Dinner € 30, by arrangement.
closed	Rarely.
directions	From Spain, through Badajoz, into Portugal for Évora. House halfway between Vila Viçosa & Monsaraz; next to castle.

António & Conchita Pimenta de Castro

tel	+351 268 459132
fax	+351 268 459155
e-mail	casadeterena@mail.telepac.pt

Monte Saraz

Horta dos Révoredos, Barrada, 7200-172 Monsaraz, Évora

Don't miss Monsaraz. This remarkably well-preserved medieval village looks out from behind lofty battlements across the plain below; at night, the silence, the narrow streets and herringbone cobbling are bewitching indeed. Down on the plain among a grove of gnarled old olives this cluster of farm buildings is a wonderful retreat. A simple white exterior (windows unusually picked out with plain black bands) belies a wonderfully rich interior, an eclectic mix of Portugal and the orient with vaulted brick ceilings. There are rugs, richly painted walls, unusual sculptural flourishes and Monique's paintings. The gardens are just as enticing with hedges and fountains merging seamlessly with orchards and groves. The swimming pool has a feel of inner sanctum cum Roman bath with wrap-around colonnade; to one end is the summer dining room with views up to Monsaraz. In the three self-contained casas (one sleeping up to seven, the others up to four) the emphasis is on a clean, simple and restful mix of whitewashed walls with some antiques, and good bedding. Supermarkets, good restaurants and all you need nearby, and just the hoot of an owl to break the silence at night. Unforgettable.

rooms	3 self-catering cottages.
price	€76 for 2. Call for full details of prices.
meals	Restaurants nearby.
closed	Rarely.
directions	From Évora, N258 for Spain to Reguengos de Monsaraz; then towards Monsaraz. Approx. 4km before Monsaraz, left at sign for 'Anta', along track. At T-junc., right; 1st house.

Monique Deckers

tel	+351 266 557385
fax	+351 266 557485
e-mail	monte.saraz@mail.telepac.pt
web	www.portugalvirtual.pt/monte.saraz

map 6   entry 99

Hotel Rural Horta da Moura

Apartado 64, Monsaraz, 7200-999 Reguengos de Monsaraz, Évora

Monsaraz is one of the treasures of the Alentejo, an ancient hilltop fortress village of cobbled streets and whitewashed walls, visible for miles and with near-circular views from its battlements of the Alentejo plains. On the slopes below lies the Horta da Moura estate, whose name recalls the Moorish invaders of the eighth century. It is a modern extension of an old house, but regional character is everywhere, with exposed stone and local slate, tiled floors strewn with rugs, and arched brick ceilings (typical of the Moors) or rustic wooden beams. Both suites and rooms are of a good size, with working fireplaces, arched ceilings and dark wood furniture. It feels immensely solid, and stout walls keep you cool indoors in the hottest weather. Do try the regional restaurant's local meat and fish, the superb local wines, as well as vegetarian food from the Swiss chef. The circular Torreão bar has a rooftop terrace where you can take the air. Here you can experience the Alentejo lifestyle, and there are added pleasures, including the games room for table tennis and the pool. If you fancy an excursion there are four horses to ride, an elegant horse-drawn carriage and bicycles.

rooms	26: 6 doubles/twins, 20 suites.
price	€85–€100; suite €100–€125.
meals	Lunch/dinner €20.
closed	Rarely.
directions	To Monsaraz; just below fortress walls, do not turn right, follow road to Mourão. Signed.

Francisco Zambujinho

tel	+351 266 550100
fax	+351 266 550108
e-mail	hortadamoura@hotmail.com
web	www.hortadamoura.pt/

Monte Alerta

Apartado 101, 7200 Monsaraz, Évora

From the garden you can see Spain in one direction and hilltop Monsaraz in the other. Monte Alerta is a classic old Alentejo farmhouse, white with blue borders to doors and windows; with its tall chimneys and roof of terracotta it sits well in this landscape of red earth, cork trees and heat haze. The inside has been professionally overhauled. Bedrooms are remarkably large, with air-conditioning a bonus in high summer. Polished tiled floors are strewn with rugs and beds have attractive covers; room 4 has lovely views of Monsaraz and the old convent; bathrooms are enormous. So too is the dining room, with long table and rustic chairs, and the games room, with big leather sofas, pool table and woodburning stove. There are no fewer than three sitting rooms, and Alentejo touches all over the place, most notably brick arches and arched *abodoba* ceilings. Everything is as clean as a new pin, beautifully cared for by friendly housekeeper Joaquina. Your hosts are delightful, and serve you three types of home-made cake at breakfast.

rooms	9: 8 doubles/twins, 1 suite.
price	€ 75; single € 60; suite € 100.
meals	Lunch/dinner (larger groups only).
closed	Rarely.
directions	From Évora to Reguengos, then follow signs to S. Pedro do Corval; on to Telhciro & look for signs to house 800m away; easy to find.

Sergio Ambrosio

tel	+351 266 550150
fax	+351 266 557325
e-mail	mail@montealerta.pt
web	www.montealerta.pt

map 6   entry 101

Casa Santos Murteira

Rua de S. Pedro 68/70/72, 7090-041 Alcáçovas, Évora

This old village house was just too good not to share. The main façade captures the eye with its exquisite wrought-iron balconies and baroque flourish above the cornicing; at its midst a guardian angel stands sentinel. The style within could be described as 'unpretentiously elegant'; the lounge is a gem with its polished parquet floor, comfy chairs, chandelier and collection of books and oils. The Virgin and Christ child look on from above the hearth. The cream and mustard dining room is just as special: light floods in from shuttered windows on two sides and there is a beautiful Arraiolos rug beneath a Queen Anne-ish dining table. Just outside is a terrace for *al fresco* meals when it is warm. The back of the house has more of an Alentejo feel with its terracotta tiles, wafer bricking and bands of blue highlighting windows and doors. A spring-fed pool sits prettily in an orange grove. There are just six bedrooms and they are among the nicest we know: fine old beds, marble-topped bedside tables, planked and rugged floors and splendidly moulded ceilings. The housekeeper works hard to make your stay memorable.

rooms	6 doubles/twins.
price	€80; single €65; family room from €75.
meals	Dinner occasionally on request.
closed	Rarely.
directions	From Évora, ring road round town until Alcáçovas signed. There, Rua de S. Pedro runs parallel to main street; house halfway up on left.

Maria da Encarnação Fernandes
tel +351 266 948220
fax +351 266 948229
e-mail contacto@montedosobral.pt
web www.montedosobral.pt

Herdade da Samarra

7090 Viana do Alentejo, Évora

José Pertana de Vasconcelos has thought of everything – even kennels for your dogs! This is a new enterprise for the organic farmer and affable host; an enthusiast about all things Alentejo he is a director of an organization promoting local produce. His is a new house, approached by an avenue of young trees, a typical *herdade* with a cool veranda looking onto a pool with palm trees and lawns. It may lack the mellow patina of age but it is an attractive building and inside is as comfortable as can be. The large sitting/dining room with bar has tiled columns and gleaming red-tiled floor. Bedrooms (air-conditioned) are coolly elegant, neat and new – a touch of *toile de Jouy* here, a polished antique there. They have bird names: the area is an orthinologist's dream. Food is regional, and home-grown lamb roasted in home-pressed olive oil could be on the menu. There's lot to see and do beside eating well and lolling by the pool: watersports on the nearby lake, castles at Alvito, Portel and Viana, Roman remains at Cucufate. As for Évora, it is so teeming with medieval monuments it has been classed a World Heritage site. *Horses available in summer.*

rooms	5 doubles/twins.
price	€ 63.
meals	Dinner € 20, on request.
closed	Rarely.
directions	From Évora for Viana do Alentejó (about 2km). Large white & yellow entrance, just off to right.

José Manuel Pertana de Vasconcelos

tel	+351 266 953670
fax	+351 266 705045
e-mail	herdsamarra@yahoo.com

map 6   entry 103

Monte do Sobral

Estrada Alcáçovas-Viana, 7090-041 Alcáçovas, Évora

Splendidly isolated and surrounded by its 300-hectare estate, Monte do Sobral is every inch the classic Alentejo farmstead: blue and white, Roman-tiled, long, low and broad-chimneyed. Most of the apartments occupy the old stable block; all have old floor tiles, a hearth, low-beamed ceilings and a small sitting room. A couple of them have a wooden mezzanine which children would love. A flock of bird prints, antlers above the hearths and animal skins on the floor reflect the owner's love of the hunt. Each of the smallish apartments has a small fridge – a useful extra in the fierce summer months. Across the way, in the main farmhouse, there is an unusual guest lounge; this too is a mezzanine affair with a small bar in one corner. Do dine at least once on the traditional country food prepared by Sobral's cheery housekeeper; it is remarkably good value. Otherwise, Alcáçovas is just a short drive away. If you tire of the pool and its long views out across the beautiful open countryside, there are a tennis court and horses to ride – even a cart that can be harnessed up, as well as mountain biking and walks across the estate. Particularly good for family holidays.

rooms	10 apartments for 2-6.
price	€45–€65 p.p.
meals	Dinner €15, on request.
closed	Rarely.
directions	From Montemor for Évora, then right for Viana. House signed to right.

Marco Fragoso Fernandes

tel	+351 266 954717
fax	+351 266 948229
e-mail	contacto@montedosobral.pt
web	www.montedosobral.pt

Monte do Chora Cascas

Turismo Rural, Apartado 296, 7050 Montemor-o-Novo, Évora

Irresistible: elegant without being stuffy, lavish without being flouncy. Sónia is welcoming and friendly – she's an architect and has designed and decorated the house with flair and imagination. She was keen to strike the right balance between hotel standards and the feel of staying in a private home – and it's worked. The bedrooms have inviting wrought-iron beds and four-posters, the very best linen, wooden ceilings and original paintings. All have lavish bathrooms. Breakfasts are generous and delicious: fresh ham, locally-produced jams, cheeses, yogurts, breads and over twenty types of tea, all served in the formal dining room. The vast sitting room has four plump blue sofas with cashmere and silk throws, an array of shapely pottery, gorgeous candles, a baby grand, an open fire and ambient music, and there's a games room with snooker and ping-pong. Outside: a courtyard with designer sunshades and loungers by the paddling pool, a shaded terrace, a tennis court and a tree house. Palm trees, fat terracotta plant pots, a ruined castle on the doorstep and great walking and mountain biking nearby; you can borrow a bike, too.

rooms	7 doubles/twins.
price	€ 75–€ 115.
meals	Restaurants nearby.
closed	Rarely.
directions	From Montemor-o-Novo, take N235 for Alcácer do Sol & follow 'Turismo Rural' signs. After 3km, right at r'bout. House on right after 800m, through security gate.

Sónia Estima Marques

tel	+351 266 899690
fax	+351 266 899699
e-mail	atendimento@montechoracascas.com
web	www.montechoracascas.com

Albergaria Solar de Monfalim

Largo da Misericórdia 1, 7000-646 Évora, Évora

Monfalim is Évora's oldest hostelry and received its first paying guest in 1892, though its history goes back to the mid-16th century. It is at the heart of beautiful old Évora on a cobbled square where huge jacaranda trees soften the urban contours; the façade is a treat with its elegant first-floor arcade built over the former stables. Pass beneath the coat of arms, climb the heavy granite staircase and emerge to meet the smartly uniformed reception staff – all to the strains of piped muzak. But fear not, this is a truly friendly hostelry and you are made to feel a valued guest at all times. Perhaps miss the lounge/TV room; choose instead a delightful little bar where old photos tell tales of the Alentejo's rural life. The dining room is large and light and leads out to the first-floor arcaded terrace where you can linger over your (buffet) breakfast. And what perfect rooms! They are high-ceilinged with old wrought-iron and brass bedsteads, lovely cotton sheets and bedspreads; old lamps, tiled floors and Arraiolos rugs add up to our type of bedroom idyll. Best time to visit? May or June, when those jacarandas bring forth their glorious purple.

rooms	26: 25 doubles/twins, 1 suite.
price	€80–€105; single €65.
meals	Restaurants nearby.
closed	Rarely.
directions	In Évora follow green tourist hotel signs. Exit ring road on Rua de Machede, via Portas de Moura, into Rua Miguel Bombarda; then right into Largo da Misericórdia.

Ana Ramalho Serrabulho

tel	+351 266 750000
fax	+351 266 742367
e-mail	reservas@monfalimtur.pt
web	www.monfalimtur.pt

Casa de Sam Pedro

Quinta de Sam Pedro, 7000-173 Évora, Évora

A delectable address, close to wonderful Évora and utterly bucolic. A sense of well-being takes hold as soon as you turn off the narrow country road and follow a winding track through old olive groves. The grand house offers a benevolent greeting; acacias throw shade across its uncluttered façade and the air is filled with birdsong. Inside, the decoration is gentle, unshowy: a grandfather clock, coats of arms, parquet floors set against old *azulejos*, gilt mirrors and the family china. The dining room is elegant but cosy, the kitchen as a great kitchen should be, the real heart of the house. We could imagine snuggling down with a good book on one of the sofas in front of the white-tiled hearth, beneath the collection of old plates and copper saucepans. (We would also choose to breakfast here – tell your host if you feel the same.) The peace of the place makes you more aware of those gently creaking floorboards as you climb to your room. Here the decoration is again subdued and utterly 'family'; perhaps a *Mater Dolorosa* above a bed, a lovely old antique wardrobe, or a fine old dressing table. Wholly authentic – this is the type of rural tourism we admire.

rooms	4 doubles/twins.
price	€ 45–€ 65.
meals	Available locally.
closed	15-30 August; 15-30 December.
directions	From Évora, Estremoz road, then follow sign to Arrailos; right at sign for Quinta da Espada. Stay on dirt track until you reach house.

Antonio Pestana de Vasconcellos

tel	+351 266 707731
fax	+351 266 752034

map 4   entry 107

Pensão Policarpo

Rua da Freiria de Baixo 16, 7000-898 Évora

This grand town mansion was built by the Counts of Lousã in the 16th century, only to be lost to the State during the purges of Pombal. It was abandoned, but then rescued some 60 years ago by the Policarpo family. They carefully set about restoration and created the most intimate of guest houses and all these years on still have buckets of enthusiasm for their work. The breakfast room is a delight; it has a high, vaulted ceiling and the three enormous windows capture the morning sunlight. The sweet sound of *fado* takes your first meal of the day into a lyrical dimension. Outside is a terrace where you can eat *al fresco* on warmer days. There is a cosy sitting room (in what once was the kitchen) with hand-painted tiles, and a part of the old town wall has been swallowed up within the house as Évora grew outwards. Bedrooms are reached via the original granite staircase; some have vaulted ceilings, many have pretty hand-painted Alentejo furniture and a number have antique bits and pieces. Ask for one with its own bathroom and a good view. A private car park is a big plus in a town of narrow streets and traffic wardens. *Note that the entrance to the car park is in Rua Conde da Serra.*

rooms	20 doubles/twins/family.
price	€ 50; single € 45; family room € 63.
meals	Restaurants nearby.
closed	Rarely.
directions	In Évora, from Lisbon, follow ring road round city until signs for Policarpo (close to university & Portas de Moura). Free car park under archway (Rua Conde da Serra da Tourega).

Michèle Policarpo

tel	+351 266 702424
fax	+351 266 702424
web	www.localnet.pt/residencialpolicarpo

Quinta da Espada
Apartado 68, Estrada de Arraiolos Km 4, 7002-501 Évora

Quinta da Espada ('of the sword' – the one hidden here by no less a man than Geraldo Geraldes, he who snatched Évora back from the Moors), surrounded by groves of olives and cork oaks and with views down to Évora, is a low, whitewashed, mimosa-graced building with ochre window surrounds and an authentic atmosphere. Bedrooms vary in size and colour scheme, with the delicately hand-painted Alentejo furniture; terracotta tiles, *estera* matting and dark beams create a rustic mood. Little touches, like towels with a hand-embroidered 'Quinta da Espada' motif, add a touch of gentility to it all. Slate is an unusual and attractive alternative in the bathrooms. The Green Room occupies what was once the (small) family chapel. We particularly liked the smaller sitting room where you breakfast and dine in front of the hearth during the colder months. You may well be tempted by the Alentejo cooking, but you can also make use of a well-equipped guest kitchen. Stay two nights and walk into Évora along tracks that lead out from the Quinta, or ramble out and explore the 12 hectare estate. But you will be forgiven for just floating in the swimming pool, perfect in hotter weather.

rooms	7: 6 doubles/twins, 1 suite.
price	€69; suite €85; single €47.50.
meals	Lunch/dinner €20, by arrangement.
closed	24-25 December.
directions	From Évora towards Arraiolos. After 4km, Quinta signed to right.

Maria Isabel Sousa Cabral
tel	+351 266 734549
fax	+351 266 736464
e-mail	quintadaespada@clix.pt
web	www.softline.pt/quintadaespada

map 4   entry 109

Monte da Serralheira

Estrada de Bairro de Almeirim, 7000-788 Évora

George and Lucia discovered the wide, open spaces of the Alentejo over 20 years ago and here they are now, farming the land just outside historic Évora and well integrated into the local community. They are still as enthralled by this wonderful country as they were in their pioneering days, and their generosity is reflected in the size and design of the apartments that occupy what once were the workers' quarters. They have their own terraces, four of them have woodburning stoves and all are high-ceilinged. They have all you need if self-catering and are cleaned every day; this could be the ideal place for a longer (family) stay. Leave guide books behind and let yourself be led by Lucia: she is a professional guide and has a number of well-documented 'circuits' out from Serralheira. And if birds are your thing, you'll be especially happy: George is an expert. You'll hear nightingales on a spring night. Horses and an instructor are available, and there's a games room. The 200-year-old farmhouse, with its large garden and terraces, exuberant bougainvillaea and wisteria, whitewashed walls offset by blue trimmings and splendidly isolated setting is a most special and peaceful place.

rooms	5 apartments for 2-4, for self-catering or B&B.
price	€48-€85.
meals	Breakfast €6. Restaurants available locally.
closed	Rarely.
directions	From Lisbon to Évora. Right onto ring road; right at r'bout next to Opel garage for Almeirim (sul). Follow road to end, to farm.

George & Lucia van der Feltz

tel	+351 266 741286
fax	+351 266 741286
e-mail	monteserralheira@mail.telepac.pt
web	www.monteserralheira.com

Parque Markádia

Apartado 17, Barragem de Odivelas, 7920-999 Alvito, Beja

Here, in the flat, open, tree-dotted Alentejo countryside, is the Parque Markádia: its potential as a recreational oasis was spotted by this dedicated Dutch couple many years ago. They fell in love with the area, the climate and the lakeside shores, resplendent with holm oaks and corks. If the thought of sweating it out under canvas at the height of summer scarcely fills you with joy, go for the cooler option: a camping site *casa*. Ten self-catering units encircle the owners' house, in a separate area from the tents – go for one of the larger ones. Décor is basic: mottled brown-tiled floors, utilitarian furniture, checked tablecloths, oven, microwave, TV... no matter: you will be spending every daylight hour outdoors, where staff are friendly and facilities all you'd expect. There's masses to do, from watersports on the freshwater lake (windsurfers, pedaloes, kayaks and row boats for hire) to tennis to swimming in the lake or two pools. Tuck into proper Portuguese food in the restaurant where a reasonable range of dishes is served, vegetarian included. A great place for an outdoor holiday that won't break the bank, and wonderful news for families.

rooms	10 self-catering apartments for 2-6.
price	Apartment per week: for 2 €250-€452; for 4 €500 €625; for 6 €685-€857.
meals	Lunch/dinner available.
closed	Rarely.
directions	Signed from N2 between Torrão & Ferreira do Alentejo. 7km from Odivelas.

Eduardo & Sofia van der Mark

tel	+351 284 763141
fax	+351 284 763102

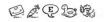

map 5   entry 111

Castelo de Milfontes

7645-234 Vila Nova de Milfontes, Beja

Carthaginians, Romans, Moors and even Algerian pirates have coveted the remarkable strategic site now held by the Castelo de Milfontes; you see why when looking out across the river estuary to the Atlantic beyond. The fort dates from the 16th century and was rescued from ruin by the family 50 years ago. This is no ordinary 'hotel' and the spirit of welcome is captured in the plaque above the hearth: *viver sem amigos não é viver* ('living without friends is not living'). Half-board is the thing at Milfontes and dinner the occasion to meet your fellow guests and Ema, who graciously presides over the table. It is an occasion to dress for: at 8pm a maid announces it is time to pass through to the dining room, where silver service and traditional Portuguese food await. The rooms have views that challenge ones descriptive powers; tower room 1 is one of the loveliest we have seen anywhere. The furniture matches the castle – perhaps an old writing desk, a baldequin bed, original oils – and all poised between vaulted ceilings and parquet floors. There is a disco across the bay in summer but a night spent here is worth small sacrifices. *Supplement for extra beds for children aged 2-15.*

rooms	7 doubles/twins. Annexe: 1 self-catering apt for 2; 1 room with kitchenette.
price	Half-board: € 155–€ 166; single € 110–€ 116. Annexe € 71 per room; single € 55.
meals	Breakfast € 5, dinner € 27. Picnic € 15.
closed	Rarely.
directions	A2 Lisbon-Grãndola. Exit before Grãndola onto IP8, for Sines. On to Cercal, then exit on N390 to V.N. de Milfontes. At edge of estuary.

Ema M. da Câmara Machado
tel +351 283 998231
fax +351 283 997122

Casa do Adro

Rua Ciario de Noticias, 10 e 10A, 7645-257 Villa Nova de Milfontes, Beja

Come in June and the Festa do Sto Antonio is on your doorstep: watch the folk-dancing from the privacy of your street-side terrace. The Casa is in the middle of town, with a castle up the road and good (fish) restaurants round the corner. Friendly and kind Doña Idalia fills the house with flowers – paper ones, silk ones and fresh blooms too; bedrooms have flower names. She has a fondness for big checks – most of the beds are covered boldly. Hers is a charmingly spruce little place, where paintwork is as fresh as a daisy and tiled floors gleam. Décor is traditionally feminine with modern touches; the dining room is Portuguese-pretty. Beds are antique or have painted headboards; one room has a terrace where pets are allowed. There's also a small kitchen for guests. Breakfasts are quite a spread, served on the terrace in summer; evening meals are typically Alentejo. Your hostess is a good cook and owns the café next door, known for its excellent cakes. Dine in town, or on the beach: the fish is as fresh as can be. And the beaches are superb, both the sheltered-estuary kind and the wild ones with waves. Don't just visit in high summer: this is a great little spot all year round. *Casas Brancas member*

rooms	6 doubles/twins.
price	€ 50-€ 75.
meals	Dinner on request.
closed	Rarely.
directions	From centre of Vila Nova de Milfontes, follow one-way system to beach, back up past castle to church, then left. House on right.

Idalia Maria Costa José

tel	+351 283 997102
fax	+351 283 997102

map 5   entry 113

Cortinhas

Vale Bejinha, 2581 Cx. S. Luis, 7630 Odemira/Milfontes, Beja

You arrive at the back, to a simple, tiny-looking house limewashed in ochre. Inside, what a surprise! It is really quite large, and opens onto a verdant terrace and veranda with views. The mood is light and sunny, with attractive colours and pale terracotta floor tiles. The large kitchen/living room is well-equipped, and has pierced metalwork doors, a sofabed, armchairs and a big wooden table. The double bedroom has powder blue walls and a patchwork quilt, the twin room a painted wood ceiling and antique beds. "I try to make it look as though someone lives here," says Sophie, and this is as far as you can get from a soulless holiday cottage. Sophie's green fingers have nurtured the climbers and fragrant herbs which encircle the house – flowers peer in through every window, you hardly know where the house ends and the garden begins. There is a splash pool close by and a small lake two minutes away. Behind, on the edge of hills, are a eucalyptus plantation, olive groves, good walks (which Tuke will guide or provide maps for) and plentiful birdlife. The coast is an easy 12km away. *Second house available in village.*

rooms	House for 4-6.
price	€60–€72; €416–€550 per week.
meals	Self-catering.
closed	Rarely.
directions	From Cercal, south towards Odemira. After S. Luis, right at cemetery (sign Val Bejinha); 2km on, right at small white cottage, up rough track, left at top.

Sophie & Tuke Taylor
tel   +351 283 976076
e-mail   walkdontwalk80@hotmail.com

Monte da Moita Nova

Apt. 4424, Cavaleiro, 7630-055 Odemira, Beja

If horse-riding and unspoilt beaches are your pleasure, stay a week with Ute and Walter at their Alentejo farm. This is an exceptionally beautiful and unspoilt part of Portugal's Atlantic coastline which has recently been designated a National Park; the eco-system of the dunes nurtures a huge variety of plant and animal life. You can reach them, and hidden coves beyond, by walking just 300 yards across Cavaleiro's pastures. The original farmhouse has two apartments and a large guest lounge; the other two have been newly built and horseshoe around a central swathe of green. They are south-facing to catch the sun; each has its own terrace and woodburner and they have a fresh and uncluttered feel: you benefit from architect Walter's good use of space. Floors are of terracotta, sheets of good linen, beds of pine, and the kitchens have full self-catering kit; they sleep two to four. The buildings are softened thanks to a riot of climbers: a wonderful spot from which to watch the sun dipping into the Atlantic. It is nice to come across a place which is so friendly to children; there are a paddling pool, beach toys and games. Ride out from Cavaleiro on well-mannered thoroughbreds.

rooms	4 apartments for 4.
price	€55 per day; €280–€485 per week.
meals	Self-catering.
closed	Rarely.
directions	From Faro IC4 via Albufeira, Portimão & Lagos. Then N120 to S. Teotónio via Aljezur, left here via Zambujeira to Cavaleiro. Here towards beach (not Cabo Sardão), & right after bridge to Moita Nova.

Ute Gerhardt

tel	+351 283 647357
fax	+351 283 647167
e-mail	moitanova@mail.telepac.pt
web	www.moita-nova.com

map 5   entry 115

Monte Fonte Nova da Telha

7630 Teotónio, Beja

Bold Moroccan colours make this place stand out. Bedrooms are great fun with bright throws on the walls, wicker furniture, colourful bedspreads and Moroccan lamps and rugs. One bedroom has a mezzanine with a double bed downstairs and twin beds up, and all rooms are spacious and light. The colours – blues, mauves, pinks, yellows, lime-greens – glow in the reflected sunlight and tell of the link between the southern Portuguese and Moorish cultures. Xica is extremely friendly and informal and adores travelling and decorating her house with unusual pieces collected along the way. This is a typical Alentejo farmhouse with a deep porch and plenty of comfortable hammocks. It is surrounded by farmland and is on the family's 20-hectare farm. The garden is very pretty, full of plants, cacti and hanging baskets; there's a barbecue and a swimming pool, too. It really is a deeply relaxing place. The dining room is ochre and saffron with a Portuguese wooden table, mirrored wall tiles and a whole wall of windows. Xica only occasionally cooks dinner but there are excellent seafood restaurants along the coast, and good beaches nearby. *Casas Brancas member.*

rooms	3 doubles.
price	€60–€80.
meals	Restaurants nearby.
closed	October–December.
directions	From São Teotónio, towards Zambujeira & after about 3km stone wall with iron gates in the eucalyptus plantation.

Maria Francisca Figueira
tel   +351 283 959159

Monte da Figueira

Vale Figueira, 7630-744 Zambujeira do Mar, Beja

Here is a spanking-new development of four holiday homes, built in the typical *monte* style, with a deep veranda running along the front. Rooms are unexpectedly large and the sloped wooden ceilings, pine shutters and doors are beautifully crafted – the whole feel is one of solidity and robustness. In traditional style floors are terracotta and walls white. The living room has a woodburner for cool nights, bathrooms are attractively tiled and the wooden kitchens are kitted out with all you need. The surrounding five hectares of flat farmland have a slightly bleak feel at present but planting will soften that; greenery thrives in this charmed climate. Swimmers are spoilt for choice, with a large, man-made lake and a new pool on site, and the captivating beaches of Zambujeira no distance away – you could even walk. Kind, helpful Miguel is the front man for the Mateus family; he speaks good English and will organize trips to the beaches and the surrounding prairies and cornfields of Litoral Alentejano. Avoid – or embrace – lively Zambujeira in August, when Portugal's answer to the Glastonbury pop festival comes to town! *Minimum stay two nights. Casas Brancas member.*

rooms	4 apartments for 2-4.
price	€ 50–€ 100.
meals	Self-catering.
closed	Rarely.
directions	Call owner on booking.

Miguel Mateus

tel	+351 917 848480
e-mail	montedafigueira@megamail.pt
web	www.casasbrancas.pt

map 5   entry 117

Monte do Papa Léguas

Alpenduradas, 7630-732 Zambujeira do Mar, Beja

Zambujeira do Mar is a small, fun place, popular with the Portuguese, drawn to its beaches like bees to a honey-pot. Stay awhile in this privileged spot: you are just a mile from the bars, restaurants, shops and beach life yet may beat an easy retreat to your quiet little corner whenever you wish. Teresa, who used to run activity holidays, is involved with them still – from this super-comfortable B&B she provides mountain bikes, helmets, water-bottles and trail maps free of charge. She can also steer you in the right direction should you be interested in canoeing, horse-riding or Atlantic cliff-top walks. The bedrooms in this rebuilt *monte* are attractive and typically Portuguese, with wooden floors, cane ceilings and calico covers on traditional iron bedsteads; fridges and TVs are neatly concealed behind little doors, and there's central heating for winter stays (much recommended). Breakfast is to be lingered over under parasols in the palm-fringed courtyard: a feast of ham, cheese, eggs and home-made jams, two types of bread, fresh juice. For those who have been up half the night acquainting themselves with the local bars, breakfast is served until 1pm. Teresa has thought of everything. *Casas Brancas member.*

rooms	5 twins.
price	€ 45-€ 70.
meals	Restaurants nearby.
closed	Rarely.
directions	From São Teotónio, follow signs to Zambujeira 2km before village, on right shortly after a road junction.

Teresa Albarran

tel	+351 283 961470
e-mail	montedopapa@sapo.pt
web	www.montedopapaleguas.com

Monte da Choça

Apartada 57, São Teotónio, 7630 S. Teotónio, Beja

If a convivial holiday is what you're after, look no further. Walkers, mountain-bikers and families would love it here, in the low-slung Alentejo *monte* overlooking the wide valley and the Monchique hills. The building has been converted into five self-catering apartments, sleeping between two and six; you live cheek-by-jowl with your neighbours – very cosy. The white-walled apartments are simply and attractively furnished, with striped rugs and cotton bedcovers adding a dash of colour. Kitchens hold all you need. A 10-minute drive west brings you to the rugged Atlantic coastline with its amazing white sandy beaches and, north, to the shops and restaurants of São Teotónio with its windy, cobbled streets. There's masses of space in which to spread your wings outdoors, good wooden seating under feathery acacia, two barbecues with big tables – and a very fine pool, with ping-pong and playground. Rodolfo, the smiling, extrovert Swiss owner, has lots of ideas on where to go and what to do; birdwatching routes and laminated maps are his specialities. No surprise to learn he plans to build a home for his family here. *Casas Brancas member.*

rooms	5 apartments.
price	€ 210–€ 560 per week.
meals	Self-catering.
closed	Rarely.
directions	From Lisbon via Sines Porto Coro Milfontes to Sâo Teotónio, take road to Odexeice & Lagos. After 4km, left at sign to Vale Juncal & through village. Continue 800m on dirt track. House ahead, through gap in high hedge.

Rudolfo Muller do Carmo

tel	+351 283 959135
fax	+351 283 959135
e-mail	contacto@montevivo.com
web	www.montevivo.com

map 5   entry 119

Cerro da Fontinha

Turismo da Natuereza Lda, Brejão, 7630-575 São Teótonio, Beja

Miguel has used only locally sourced, natural and traditional materials in these unique self-catering cottages. The simple character of the peasant dwellings has been kept, while funky, chunky and even wacky touches have been added. And to reveal the different building methods Miguel has left visible areas of *taipa* so you can see the mix of soil and stones between lath and plaster. Everything is as natural as can be: showers have stone bases and terracotta surrounds; a bunk bed has a carved ladder and fat wooden legs. Hooks for coats, towels and lavatory rolls have been created by embedding pebbles in the walls. Thick chunks of wood become mantelpieces, sofas have stone bases (covered with comfy cushions!), beds are of solid wood. Kitchen work surfaces curve, there are little alcoves for oil and vinegar, and lots of cheerful stripes and gingham. You have countryside on the doorstep, a eucalyptus wood for shade, good restaurants and Carcalhal beach nearby — you can hire mountain bikes to get there. There's also a little lake for swimming and fishing, and a communal seating area as well as private seating for each house. Astonishing and inspiring. *Minimum two nights.*

rooms	2 self-catering cottages for 4.
price	€90–€160 for 2 nights; €280–€560 per week.
meals	Restaurants nearby.
closed	Rarely.
directions	From Faro A22 (IPI) to Lagos, then the N120 through Aljezur for São Teótonio. 5km after crossing into Alentejo, left to Brejão, then 1st left. House on right just after lake.

Miguel Godinho

tel	+351 282 949083
fax	+351 282 949083
e-mail	cfontinha@sapo.pt
web	www.cerrodafontinha.com

Quinta do Barranco da Estrada
7665-880 Santa Clara a Velha, Beja

Hugging the shore of one of the Alentejo's largest freshwater lakes, the Quinta is ideal if you love wild beauty and are looking for a real hideaway. The whole area has a micro-climate which keeps the water warm enough for a long swimming season and nurtures an amazing range of plant and animal life; visit in spring and the wild flowers will have you in raptures. Lulu and Frank spent a decade renovating the original low house and then added a row of guest rooms. They are light, cool and uncluttered and their terraces look towards the lake. Lounge, dining room and bar share one large room and happily embrace Portuguese and English styles of décor. Beyond huge windows there is a vine-festooned terrace where you spend most of your time when it's warm. Above the lake a series of terraces has been planted with hibiscus, oleander, palm, jasmine, plumbago and cactus. A sinuous path cuts down through all this to the jetty where you can canoe, fish for crayfish, sail, water-ski or walk the shoreline, perhaps in the company of one of the McClintocks' six dogs. Frank will help with the naming of all those birds and, if you're lucky, you may see mongoose or wild boar. *Casas Brancas member.*

rooms	8: 7 doubles/twins, 1 family room.
price	€90–€145; single €75–€135; family room €175–€300.
meals	Cooked breakfast €10; lunch €15; dinner €25.
closed	Mid-November–mid-February.
directions	From S. Martinho das Amoreiras, head towards Portimão. At T-junc., left to Monchique; after 8km left to Cortes Pereiras; after 8.5km right to Quinta.

Lulu & Frank McClintock

tel	+351 283 933065
fax	+351 283 933066
e-mail	paradiseinportugal@mail.telepac.pt
web	www.paradise-in-portugal.com

map 5   entry 121

Herdade da Matinha

7555-231 Cercal do Alentejo, Setúbal

This is a classic Alentejo farmhouse; long, low and encircled by the striking russet-brown trunks of the cork oak. Yet though the setting is deeply rural you are close to the wonders of the protected Costa Vicentina and to the towns of Cercal and Vila Nova de Milfontes. Monica works part of the year as a tourist guide and will help plan your sorties; Alfredo is an artist and looks after the cooking. He loves to chat with guests in the kitchen while preparing meals, usually to classical or baroque music. His paintings add life and colour to the lounge which is large, light and comfortable and which leads to a terrace where camellias give way to groves of citrus – a lovely spot for meals when it's warm. Centre stage at Matinha is the kitchen with a big wooden table where you eat breakfast *en famille* and where dinner promises "the best traditional dishes but healthier than usual" (i.e. with more and better-prepared vegetables). Bedrooms are large, uncluttered, slate-floored and home to more of Alfredo's paintings; furnishings have a Conran feel. Come for the utter peace, an interesting mixture of 'trad' Portugal with modern elements, and to meet your polyglot hosts.

rooms	8 twins.
price	€ 70–€ 90; single (low season only) € 60–€ 80.
meals	Dinner € 25.
closed	Rarely.
directions	From Lisbon A2, exit Beja-Ferreira, then for Algarve-Ourique. At Mimosa, right to Alvalade-Cercal. At Cercal to Vila Nova de Milfontes. House signed, right. Follow track for 3km.

Alfredo Moreira da Silva

tel	+351 269 949247
fax	+351 269 949247
e-mail	info@herdadedamatinha.com
web	www.herdadedamatinha.com

Verdemar

Casas Novas, 7555-026 Cercal do Alentejo, Setúbal

Although only a short drive from the Atlantic beaches, Verdemar's setting is bucolic. Hidden away among stands of old cork oaks beyond the blue and white main gate a very special country retreat awaits. Guest rooms are spread around the outbuildings but the focus is the main farmhouse and dining room (see photo). The atmosphere is easy and cosy; a wooden beamed ceiling, an open kitchen/bar, wooden stools and chairs. You'll share fun and good food around one big table – *al fresco* in summer. Nuno, a professional chef for 20 years in Amsterdam, loves to share your company as he prepares dinner and exchange a recipe or two. Leading off the kitchen, the lounge, equally cosy with guitar, paintings, an old lamp; a cool place to escape summer heat. And it is heartening to find somewhere so ready to welcome families; young children will meet ducks, chickens, donkeys, cows and sheep and can have a high tea. Bedrooms are just right: no hotel extras but nothing lacking. There is a very attractive swimming pool, too, fenced off for the safety of children. Our type of idyll – with the true spirit of honest hostelry. *Casas Brancas member.*

rooms	5 doubles/twins; 3 self-catering cottages.
price	From € 75; cottages from € 70.
meals	Dinner € 21, on request (not Sun).
closed	Rarely.
directions	From Lisbon A2, exit Beja Ferreira, then N262 for Algarve. 500m after Mimosa, right for Cercal. 7km before Cercal, house signed up track on left.

Nuno Vilas-Boas & Christine Nijhoff

tel	+351 269 904544
fax	+351 269 904544
e-mail	verdemar.cercal@mail.telepac.pt
web	www.verdemar.net

map 5   entry 123

Inn Albergeria Bica-Boa

Estrada de Lisboa 266, 8550 Monchique, Faro

Healing, visualisation, massage and meditation are among the offerings at Bica Boa, as is a good selection of vegetarian food and delicious breakfasts, thanks to Susan, who has lived here for years. Bica Boa's name was inspired by the springs that well up on this wooded mountainside above Monchique; winding your way up from the western Algarve the exuberant vegetation of the place takes you by surprise. There are stunning walks galore; if you venture up here, do stay at this peaceful inn. Though it stands just to the side of the road there is little traffic and the four guest rooms are tucked away to the rear. They are fresh, light and simply decorated with wooden floors and ceilings, and all have super-comfortable beds and views across the valley. There is a quiet little guest lounge with the same view; a corner chimney, *azulejo*-clad walls and a chess table give a homely feel. Bica Boa's restaurant is popular with locals and ex-pats up from the coast. Susan even has a five-day detox programme on the menu! There are terraces for *al fresco* dining when the weather is right and a terraced garden with quiet corners for sitting out – and a beautiful young collie and black Lab, too. *Reiki healing and courses available.*

rooms	4: 3 doubles, 1 suite.
price	€53–€63; suite €125–€175.
meals	Lunch/dinner available, €15–€20.
closed	Rarely.
directions	From Faro, N125 west for Lagos. Exit for Monchique. Follow signs for Lisboa through town. Inn approx. 300m after town on right, signed.

Susan Clare Cassidy

tel	+351 282 912271
fax	+351 282 912360
e-mail	enigma@mail.telepac.pt

Monte Rosa

Lagoa da Rosa, 8600-016 Barão de S. João, Faro

Arianne loves to show other children the garden at Monte Rosa, the old farm complex run by her mother Sandra. In these three hectares of flourishing Algarve hinterland you can self-cater, go B&B... or camp under the almond, olive and fig trees. Sandra is Dutch and has converted the farmhouse and outbuildings into apartments and rooms – the result is a well-organised, informal and friendly rural holiday home. All the bedrooms are simple and attractive, with lots of wood. For those living under canvas – or in camper van – there's a kitchen to share. Near the house is a colourful garden with pathways, terraces, playground and little saltwater pool; children will also love the cats, chickens, hamsters and rabbit. Sandra used to run a restaurant in Lagos and the food is delicious; four nights a week she cooks Portuguese, international and vegetarian dinners. The communal room is where you eat, with bar, pretty pale terracotta sofas that match the floor, and ochre-sponged paintwork. There's also a sun terrace for morning meditation, a village with grocery store and restaurants nearby, and babysitting can be arranged. A wonderfully informal set-up, perfect for families.

rooms	7: 5 doubles/twins, 1 single, 1 family room. Also 2 apts for 4-8.
price	€ 45-€ 50; single € 35-€ 45; family € 60; apartment € 80.
meals	Dinner € 15, with wine.
closed	Rarely.
directions	From Lagos for Aljezur/Bensafrim; after 2km through Portelas; at end of village left to Barão de S. João. House 6km on left.

Sandra Falkena

tel	+351 282 687002
fax	+351 282 687015
e-mail	monte.rosa@clix.pt
web	www.monterosaportugal.com

map 5　entry 125

Salsalito

Estrada da Luz, Burgau, 8600-146 Lagos, Faro

A dream home that Ralph and Sally have spent some years creating – it's high-quality 'Santa Fe', rustic in style, with chunky wood beams, half-tree trunk shelves and curious 'junk' collections. The guest book tells it like it is: "perfect", "wonderful" and "award yourself 20 stars". Sally will read your cards at the drop of a hat and Ralph is a master of all trades, including carpentry. He recycled timber to make wardrobes, tables and door lintels. The lounge has a beamed ceiling and log fire for cooler nights. The top terrace honesty bar is well stocked; only teetotallers will fail to enjoy its – and your hosts' – abundance. On hotter days, you can relax in the horseshoe-shaped cloister with bamboo seats and wooden ceiling festooned with bougainvillaea… nearby, among attractive mixed trees, is a stunning new pool circled by sunloungers and a tropical rock waterfall. The bedrooms have a touch of British B&B, with kettles and teabags; the newest, in a converted outbuilding, is painted a sunny yellow and is Mexican in style. You'll find plenty to do here: Burgau, with its bars and restaurants, is only two minutes by car and still retains its lovely old fishing village character. *Minimum three nights.*

rooms	4 doubles/twins.
price	€35–€40; £235 per week.
meals	Restaurants nearby.
closed	November–March.
directions	Left off N125 for Almadena, then towards Burgau. Look out for yellow balustrade, right immediately. If you reach the Pig's Head, you've gone too far.

Ralph & Sally Eveleigh

tel	+351 282 697628
fax	+351 282 788272
e-mail	salsalito@clix.pt
web	www.algarve-salsalito.com

Quintinha de Nova
Barrocal, Nr. Messines, Faro

The gallery library in this rambling Algarve farmhouse has a bamboo ceiling, curved windows, comfortable armchairs, paintings, CDs and a wall of books – you'll feel very at home. And there's a garden, a flower-filled patio, a swimming pool and lots of shady spots – perfect for a family. The vast dining room with wooden table, carved chairs and quirky chandelier made from a mule cartwheel was once the cow barn; now the old mangers hold Portuguese and English pottery. You can prepare all you need in the well-furnished kitchen. Nova, who lives in Scotland, adores Portuguese ceramics and exports them, along with local honey and lavender, to her Scottish farm shop. You have four double bedrooms, one with its own bath, and two shared showers; one room is particularly lovely, a good size and prettily tiled, with lacy and hand-embroidered little cushions on the bed. Maria lives next door and looks after the place – she is delightful and pops in to feed the two cats and to have a chat. The large walled garden has a barbecue, lots of trees and fragrant herbs; there's a picturesque cart in one corner and a hammock in the other. Countryside enfolds you, yet you are very close to Faro.

rooms	Self-catering house for 8.
price	£525–£1,596 per week.
meals	Restaurants nearby.
closed	Rarely.
directions	From Faro, A22 to Boliqueime. Through Paderne for Messines, then turn off for Barrocal. Follow signs to Mouricão & quinta on road.

Nova Gourlay

tel	+44 (0)1273 747811
fax	+44 (0)1273 329344
e-mail	rentals@thevillaagency.co.uk

map 5   entry 127

Quinta da Alfarrobeira

Estrada do Palmares, Odiáxere, 8600-252 Lagos, Faro

For the young family from Holland, now embellishing their dream home, it was love at first sight. Quinta da Alfarrobeira stands on a hill just inland from the Algarve coast and is surrounded by six hectares of old fruit groves. You might be fired by similar dreams as you sit beneath the enormous *alfarrobeira* (carob) and gaze out across the old olive and almond trees, or watch the family's three sons playing happily with their adopted pets on a sunny flower-filled patio. Choose between the room in the main house, with own bathroom, and one of two guest houses built in traditional Algarve style where terracotta, beam and bamboo are the essential ingredients. We loved their light, airy feel and the antique furnishings that have been collected piecemeal from all over Europe. There are biggish bathrooms, private terraces and views – and kitchens in the guest houses if you plan to cook for yourself. Add to this the lovely walks out from the Quinta (just a mile down to the sea), exceptionally kind hosts and you might find you never want to leave. *Minimum stay three nights.*

rooms	1 double; 2 self-catering houses.
price	€50–€70; 'Stable' €60–€100; 'Farmhouse' €75–€140.
meals	Available locally.
closed	Rarely.
directions	From Faro E1, then N125 to Portimão & on for Lagos. In Odiáxere, left at square for Meia Praia & Palmares. After 1.3km (cow sign on right), left. 1st house on right.

Theo Bakker & Inge Keizer

tel	+351 282 798424
fax	+351 282 799630
e–mail	bakker@mail.telepac.pt

Quinta das Barradas
Odiáxere, 8600-255 Lagos, Faro

Almost hidden in the agricultural landscape is this large farm with converted barns and outbuildings. It's beautiful, elegant and comfortable and is professionally run by hoteliers Urs and Vera, a friendly and gracious couple. Wherever you look there is creative use of materials – carved stone, wood, old roof tiles, flagstones, cobbles. The main house is like a Minho farmhouse, yet sits perfectly in this Algarve landscape. Bedrooms are traditional with tiled floors, scrolled wooden beds, wooden ceilings and excellent bathrooms. Each room has its own sitting area outside, so you have space and privacy. The food is delicious and served on a heavy table in a room with a flagstone floor and candelabra; outside is a covered eating area. The Swiss chef offers international and Portuguese dishes, and a three-course dinner; most of the food is home-produced or local. Palm and fruit trees surround the farm and there's a spring which feeds pools via reed beds, plus a natural swimming pool. Horse-riding is available at English stables nearby.

rooms	15 doubles/twins.
price	€96; single €58.
meals	Dinner, €20-€30 (not Sun/Mon).
closed	Rarely.
directions	From Odiáxere out of village to *barragem*; at windmill, fork right, downhill for 400m, then 1st left (very small sign) to end.

Urs & Vera Wild

tel	+351 282 770200
fax	+351 282 770209
e-mail	quintabarradas@vivendamiranda.pt

map 5   entry 129

Quinta das Achadas

Estrada da Barragem, Odiáxere, 8600-251 Lagos, Faro

Hats off to attentive new owners Júlio and Jill: the Quinta remains one of the most idyllic B&Bs of the Algarve. The approach is a delight, a winding drive through groves of olive, almond and orange trees which give way to a wonderful subtropical garden where maguey and palm, geranium and bourgainvillea, pine and jasmine jostle for position; there's a heated, salt-water pool too, a *cabana* with 'honesty' bar, a hydro-massage jacuzzi and a small children's playground. The bedrooms, each with its own small terrace, look out across the gardens and are in a converted barn and stables. They are Algarve-rustic, with wooden ceilings, white walls, modern art and beautiful country antiques. Gorgeous bathrooms come with Santa Katerina tiles and swish showers. In colder weather you breakfast in a cosy dining room but most of the year it's mild enough to sit out on the huge terrace with views. You can self-cater in the apartments. Dinners are three-course, eclectic and very good; your hosts, who used to work in the restaurant trade, combine professionalism with a warm, human touch. *Minimum three-day stay in apartments.*

rooms	3 doubles/twins; 3 self-catering apartments, for 2-4.
price	€70–€90; apartment €95–€160.
meals	Dinner €25, with wine (2-3 times a week).
closed	Rarely.
directions	From Portimão, N125 for Lagos. In Odiáxere, right at sign for *barragem*. House signed on right after 1.2km.

Jill & Júlio & Isabella Pires

tel	+351 282 798425
fax	+351 282 799162
e-mail	info@algarveholiday.net
web	www.algarveholiday.net

Casa Colina
Mont Fonseca, Burgau, Faro

The hills are silent – you are completely secluded among the fig-trees, yet only a two-minute drive from the sea. The single-story farmhouse, typical of the region, is 200 years old and reveals touches of Roger's artistic flair. He is a painter and journalist and unusual in being so easy about sharing his peaceful space. If you want to paint, feel free to borrow an easel and head for the studio. There's a whole stack of art books, some beautiful plates collected at gypsy markets and a fascinating collection of old bottles, Robert has written a book about them – including one 18th-century water bottle filled with quinine and white port used to cure a fever. The studio overflows with abstract and colourful paintings – this obviously encourages creativity. There are two self-catering studios: the cosy 'Picasso' is perfect for a couple; its open-plan bedroom/lounge has a beamed ceiling, red tiled floors, a woodburning stove, antique furniture, red throws and rugs and several arches. 'Matisse' is much larger, with two bedrooms and the same rustic and fresh feel; both share a pretty terrace and tropical garden with climbers, cacti and ferns. The fishing village of Burgau is only a short walk away.

rooms	2 self-catering apartments.
price	€ 234–€ 593 per week.
meals	Restaurants nearby.
closed	Rarely.
directions	From Faro, A22 & IP1 to Lagos & Sagres; after Almadena left to Burgau. Look for sports centre on right & shortly after, right (on a bad bend) onto dirt track. Continue until sign; furthest half of house.

Roger Green

tel	+351 282 697518
fax	+351 282 697518
e-mail	rogerwords@clix.pt

map 5   entry 131

Casa da Palmeirinha

Rua da Igreja, 1, Mexilhoeira Grande, 8500-132 Portimão, Faro

This graceful old house, centred on its inner courtyard and garden, may remind you of houses of Seville or Morocco; it is also bigger than it seems from the outside. José, a newspaper columnist who speaks excellent English, is an entirely genial host and was born here; the house was his grandfather's. The bedrooms have varied views of the church and village; our two favourites have access to a terrace and roof garden with views of the Alvor bird sanctuary. The Spanish-influenced sitting room has walls decorated with dark green and white tiles, a terracotta floor and rustic wooden furniture. Then there's the huge interior tiled patio with its ornamental pool, swimming pool and lawn, shaded by arching palms – a superb place to relax. You are free to make tea and coffee in the kitchen. This is an unusual opportunity to stay in a truly Portuguese 'townhouse' that is a delight inside and out. The village too is genuinely Portuguese-Algarve and has the famous Vila Lisa restaurant. There's the bird sanctuary nearby, and good walks – you may well meet the owners' friendly old Algarve water dogs and Labrador.

rooms	5 doubles/twins/family.
price	€60–€80; single €50–€60; family room €77–€97.
meals	Restaurants nearby.
closed	December.
directions	From Portimão or Lagos on N125; into Mexilhoeira Grande to church. House on left, turn left.

José Manuel Júdice Glória

tel	+351 282 969277
fax	+351 282 969277
e-mail	josejudice@mail.telepac.pt

Quinta das Flores
Vale de Dega, Mexilhoeira Grande, Figueira, 8500 Portimão, Faro

There is art in the very fabric of the colourful Quinta of Flowers – Gaelle and David, who farmed in Africa, are also landscape gardener and painter. The sculpted gardens have beautiful lawns, palms, pergolas of bougainvillaea and shady spots, and there's a tennis court, a curved pool, a barbecue and a bar. The interior of the elegant Algarve house has a colonial feel, thanks partly to Gaelle's vibrant paintings of zebras and her landscapes of Africa and the Alentejo. The galleried sitting room is warm with terracotta floors strewn with rugs, cream walls, large, comfy sofas and chairs and honesty bar, and there are open fires for cooler seasons. There are also large wicker armchairs overlooking the garden. The Pool Room is a double with shower, two steps from the swimming pool. You can self-cater in the grounds, too: in the cottage, with double and twin bedrooms, or the studio. The décor is fresh and sunny, the beds are large and the atmosphere homely. Gaelle prepares everything from Thai and Indian curries to vegetarian food to typical Portuguese, served in the large, green-painted dining room. Breakfasts can be full English or continental – you choose.

rooms	1 double; 1 self-catering studio; 1 cottage for 4.
price	€ 65; studio € 65; cottage€ 665 (per week).
meals	Lunch/dinner by arrangement.
closed	Rarely.
directions	From Portimão, to Lagos, past Penina, right into Figueira. Past church & just before pink Café Célia, right.

Gaelle & David Hamp-Adams

tel	+351 282 968649
fax	+351 282 969293
e-mail	ghampadams@hotmail.com

map 5   entry 133

Casa Três Palmeiras
Apartado 84, 8501-909 Portimão, Faro

What a setting! From the Casa's perch right at the cliff's edge the view is a symphony of sea, sky, and rock — ever-changing according to the day's mood and ever beautiful. The house was built in the Sixties, but the Zen design still feels modern. It has a distinctly exotic feel thanks to three enormous palm trees and the simple arches that soften the façade and give welcome shade to the guest rooms once the temperature climbs. Rooms have everything you might expect for the price. There are marble floors, double sinks and big, fitted wardrobes, yet they remain beautifully uncluttered. Best of all, they lead straight out onto the terrace — whence those heavenly views — and sea-water pool. It is a very comfortable house and the service is warm and friendly. There are always freshly cut flowers and a bowl of fruit for you and it is obvious that entertaining comes naturally to Dolly, a Brazilian. A path leads from the house straight down to the beach; get up early and you may find you have it to yourself — even in midsummer. Book well ahead in July/August. *Reduced green fees and car hire rates available for guests.*

rooms	5 doubles/twins.
price	€ 194; single € 172.
meals	Snacks available.
closed	December–February.
directions	From Portimão, dual carriageway for Praia da Rocha. Right at last r'bout for Praia do Vau; at next r'bout double back & turn up track on right after 100m. Right along track at 1st villa.

Dolly Schlingensiepen

tel	+351 282 401275
fax	+351 282 401029
e-mail	dolly@casatrespalmeiras.com
web	www.casatrespalmeiras.com

Casa Domilu

Estrada de Benagil, Alfanzina, 8400 Carvoeiro, Faro

This small, newish resort-hotel flaunts its frills at every turn. If neo-Doric columns and musak are not your thing, stay away... But if you secretly hanker after a glitzy place to stay on the Algarve, then you will love it! The décor of lounge and dining room is pick-and-mix: repro antiques, Art-Deco-ish chairs, glass-topped tables, dragon-tooth floors. Bedrooms are big, light, cheerful and marble-floored and have all the extras: book the honeymoon suite and you get a sunken whirlpool bath surrounded by potted palms. Outside, sweeping colonnaded steps lead to a fabulous new palm-studded terrace with curvaceous pool and children's pool; new bedrooms too. The saltwater indoor pool, with jacuzzi, is equally gorgeous. Breakfast is buffet, big and designed to please a northern European palate, while dinner (candlelit) is resolutely Portuguese. There is tennis – floodlit at night – a gymnasium, sauna and beauty spa, and mountain bikes; beaches and golf courses are a saunter away. Guests, many of whom are German, return year after year.

rooms	30: 24 doubles/twins, 6 suites.
price	Doubles/twins €59–€131; suite €120–€219.
meals	Dinner €20.
closed	Rarely.
directions	From N125, exit for Carvoeiro. 200m after Intermarché supermarket, left at signs for house.

Abilio D'Almeida

tel	+351 282 350610
fax	+351 282 358410
e-mail	casa.domilu@mail.telepac.pt
web	www.casa-domilu.com

map 5   entry 135

Casa Belaventura

Campina de Boliqueime, 8100-073 Loulé, Faro

Belaventura lies deep in the Algarve hinterland, in such a pastoral setting you will soon forget that the highway and the busy coastal towns of Vilamoura and Albufeira are close by. Carlos converted this old farmhouse with B&B and self-catering in mind; as well as a beautifully proportioned sitting room there is a large dining room and a fully equipped kitchen. The house is light and airy from the open arches that link the spaces; a more traditional Algarve style is present in the terracotta floor, wafer brickwork and marvellously weathered roof tiles. Carlos has given the building extra volume and more modern lines by extending the roof outwards thus creating a shady outside sitting area. By the pool in the garden there's a hammock in the shade of an olive tree; beyond, through the almond groves, you catch glimpses of the glittering sea. The bedrooms have contemporary paintings (some by Carlos's wife), durries, more traditional beam and bamboo roofs, perhaps a rattan chair or view across the garden. One is more of a suite with its own sitting room and inglenook. Carlos has a boat and can take you for a day's sailing along the Algarve coast. *Note 20% supplement during public holidays.*

rooms	4: 3 doubles/twins, 1 suite.
price	€75–€100; single €65–€90. Whole house, self-catering, €1,750–€2,750 per week.
meals	Restaurants nearby.
closed	November–February.
directions	From Faro, IP1 for Spain. Exit for Boliqueime, after 250m, right. House signed on right after approx. 750m.

Carlos Jorge Dias

tel	+351 289 360633
fax	+351 289 366053
e-mail	belaventura@mail.telepac.pt

Kazuri Garden Cottages

8100 Loulé, Faro

In a lush valley in the Algarve just a couple of miles back from the coast, long hours of sunshine and rich soil allow nearly everything to grow in profusion. The English owner found this old wine farm in ruins in the early 70s and has put in years of patient restoration and planting. This is a place of peace and privacy; behind the whitewashed outer wall the cottages stand apart from one another facing the gardens and – tucked away beyond – is an enormous round swimming pool. Each cottage has a sun and a shade terrace, a tiled kitchen, a sitting room and double bedroom – perfect for two. (The cottages are self-catering, but breakfast is also available.) Dried flowers, eucalyptus beams and terracotta give a 'country' feel, while mementos from Africa and Turkey add an exotic note. There are magazines and a carefully compiled file with details of restaurants, shops and visits. What we remember most are the gardens: olive, pomegranate, almonds and lemon and, beneath them, a profusion of flowers of every hue. The benign climate means that visiting out of season is just as special. *Car hire can be arranged in the UK.*

rooms	6 self-catering cottages for 2.
price	£200-£500 per week.
meals	Restaurants nearby.
closed	Rarely.
directions	Information will be sent by UK agent (see below).

E S Wiltsher

tel	+ 44 (0)1642 714623 (UK agent)
fax	+ 44 (0)1642 710226

map 5   entry 137

Casa da Calma

Sitio do Pereiro, 327 x, Moncarapacho/Olhão, 8700-123 Moncarapacho, Faro

Pick your own oranges for breakfast! Nicole's small hotel, established two years ago in the unspoiled Algarve hills, is surrounded by amazingly verdant gardens and lawns. Hospitality runs in the family: German-born Nicole worked in the tourist industry for several years and her mother, who is House Cook, once ran a Californian guest house. Décor at the renovated farm is hotel-comfortable but not hotel-anonymous and each bedroom is different: matching paisley bedcovers and curtains in one, wooden Portuguese beds in another. All have ceiling fans, their own generous terraces and thoughtful extras like fluffy white bathrobes and poolside towels. Breakfasts – brunches too – are quite a spread. The poolside is decked with yellow-cushioned loungers and jolly parasols, and there's a sauna. Further afield lie the fantastic island beaches of Armona and Tavira. Your hostess is an expert when it comes to organizing trips – horse-riding, sailing, fishing, water-skiing and jeep safaris are all within your grasp. Nicole understands the importance of a little retail therapy too and will organize shopping trips to Lisbon, or over the border to stunning Seville.

rooms	7 doubles/twins (2 can be linked to make a suite or family room).
price	€92-€138; single €58-€68; suite €200-€240.
meals	Dinner €15-€20, by arrangement.
closed	Rarely.
directions	Faro IP1 for Spain. Exit Olhão, Sta Caterina & Moncarapacho. Then towards Sta Catarina. House on left after 2km.

Nicole Effenberg

tel	+351 289 791098
fax	+351 289 791599
e-mail	nicole.effenberg@clix.pt
web	www.casadacalma.com

Pedras Verdes Guesthouse

Sítio da Boavista, CP 658 T Quelfes, 8700 Olhão, Faro

The house is low and north-African style, surrounded by carob and olive trees. The bedrooms are all different and all sensational. Each has a theme: baroque, African, Asiatic, Zen, Arabic. There are funky walk-in showers with pebbled or wooden flooring, plain walls, minimalist décor, Portuguese antiques and some modern pieces. The Asiatic room has fresh palms, lime green bedcovers and ceiling nets over the bed. The little touches make a real impact and each key has a symbol – a cowrie shell for the Asiatic room, an ebony sculpted head for the African room. Artistically placed fruit in the bedrooms, sweets, fresh flowers and postcards. The humour in the décor reflects the character of the lovely owners – Muriel and André are genuinely welcoming and very enthusiastic about creating a beautiful space. The same minimalist and stylish feel extends to the garden where stone sculptures are filled with exotic shells and crystals. You can relax by the divine pool or under the canvas canopy. There is an overriding sense of calm and peace here. Dinner is served on a beautiful wooden table, and is French and delicious, and the cocktails are sublime.

rooms	6 doubles/twins.
price	€80–€95.
meals	Lunch €6–€7; dinner €11–€14, by request. Closed Mondays.
closed	Rarely.
directions	From Faro airport IC4 to São Bras; on to N2 A22 to Spain; exit 15 Olhão O 'Quelfes'. Entering village, sharp left-hand bend at white building with red base; sharp right, follow green stones (or phone & André will meet you.)

Muriel & André Mandi

tel	+351 289 721343
fax	+351 289 721343
e-mail	info@pedrasverdes.com
web	www.pedrasverdes.com

map 6   entry 139

Quinta da Belgica

Sítio da Fornalha, 8700 Moncarapacho, Faro

Almost hidden by luxuriant trees and climbers, this two-storey, purpose-built holiday complex is perfect for families with young children. The atmosphere created by Mieke and Jef is casual and relaxed and since they moved here four years ago they have been steadily brightening up the rooms. Bedrooms are basic rather than luxurious, with tiled floors, stripey curtains and aluminium doors which double as windows; half are now air-conditioned. But you probably won't spend much time indoors when life revolves around the pool and gardens. There is almost a hectare of grounds here with masses of flowers and plenty of shady spots beneath palm, orange, almond and pepper trees. There are outdoor tables shaded by a bamboo roof and, near the pool, the combined bar, lounge and dining room, with big squashy sofa and armchairs – and a woodburning stove for cool evenings. Mieke cooks both Portuguese and northern European dishes. For entertainment there's ping-pong and table football and even a collection of dressing-up clothes for the children. The beaches are five kilometres away.

rooms	17: 11 doubles/twins, 6 family rooms.
price	€ 60–€ 110.
meals	Dinner € 25.
closed	January–mid-February.
directions	From Moncarapacho to Olhão. After sharp bend, entrance marked with flags.

Mieke & Jef Everaert & Cloots
tel	+351 289 791193
fax	+351 289 791192
e-mail	info@quinta-da-belgica.com
web	www.quinta-da-belgica.com

Mad Manor

Vale das Amoreiras, Lote 7 Alcalar, 8500-120 Mexilhoeira Grande, Faro

A great alternative to renting your own villa – and you don't even have to make breakfast. Your delightful hosts will book things up for you, too: golf, riding, surfing, tennis. The large and stately white villa is one of a development of eight, each in an oleander – and hibiscus-filled garden. You have your own marble-floored suite of rooms and will feel most spoilt. The main bedroom, with blue carpeting and white walls, satin bedcovers, soft lighting and swagged curtain has lovely views of the Monchique hills. The other bedrooms, two twins, are pretty with pine furniture and rugs; the bathroom, with 'his' and 'hers' basins, is big and shared. In the kitchen are fridge, kettle, toaster and microwave so you can prepare your own snacks and drinks, and there's an 'honesty' table of drinks, too. The lounge/dining room leads onto a terrace with lovely views. Angela and David, who live downstairs, are happy for you to join them for barbecues in the evenings; if you prefer to eat out, the restaurants in the village are a walk away. The large and lovely pool – yours to share – is the colour of the Algarve sky. All this, and those glorious white sand beaches a four-wheel sprint away.

rooms	1 apartment for 2-6.
price	€ 80 double; € 40 extra room.
meals	Breakfast included. Restaurants nearby.
closed	Rarely.
directions	From m'way at Alvor, EN125 to Lagos. 1st right after BP petrol station to Alcalar. Under railway, over m'way, past Alcalar until sign 'Monumentos Megalithicos'. Right, then 1st left. 2nd house on left.

David Broad

tel	+351 282 471530
fax	+351 282 470359
e-mail	madmanor@mail.telepac.pt
web	www.mad-manor.com

map 5   entry 141

Quinta da Lua

Bernardinheiro 1622-X, S. Estevão, 8800-513 Tavira, Faro

Miguel and Vimal have stacks of enthusiasm and love looking after people; staying at the 'Farm of the Moon' is delightful on many levels. The food is especially good; Vimal is a professional chef who cooks 'global kitchen' and Mediterranean, including imaginative vegetarian dishes. Breakfast is different every day, and guests are asked their preferences; we noticed one enjoying beautifully arranged fruit one morning while sitting out under the green umbrella. The house is a two-storey addition to an old Algarve farmhouse, surrounded by orange trees and vineyards, carob, oleander, bougainvillaea and palms; there is a lovely pool with shaded verandas to the the side. Inside is a highly successful blend of modern and traditional décor, with rough terracotta floor tiles and beamed ceilings throughout. Delicious bedrooms have white walls, generous beds and are well-insulated against noise. The moon logo is duplicated in two colours in bathrooms, so you won't borrow your room-mate's towel by mistake! It is a delightful surprise to find such a special place so close to the island beaches – good local restaurants, too – run by such nice people.

rooms	8: 6 doubles/twins, 2 suites.
price	€ 80; suite € 100.
meals	Lunch/dinner € 17 (1-2 times a week).
closed	10 November–15 December.
directions	From Faro, IP1 to Spain, exit Tavira. At 2nd r'bout, N125 for Olhão. Right to S. Estevão. 1st left & next right, & look for arch over Quinta gateway.

Miguel Martins & Vimal Willems

tel	+351 281 961070
fax	+351 281 961070
e-mail	quintadalua@iol.pt
web	www.quintadalua.com

Convento de Santo António

Rua de Santo António 56, 8800-705 Tavira, Faro

What a surprise! An inauspicious area, but seek out a tiny door in the ancient wooden gate by the chapel... it leads, incredibly, to this dazzling white convent surrounded by banana plants and a lazy pool. Isabel is almost apologetic that "the home has only been in the family for five generations". A portrait of great-grandmother gazes down one of the vaulted corridors that runs the length of the cloister while Santo António looks on benignly from his chapel at the end of the other. It was grandfather, much travelled, who planted the exotic garden. The bedrooms vary in size (and price) and have a convent-like charm: here a vaulted ceiling, there a fine dresser; here a seaward view, there a hand-knotted rug. It is a Lusitanian feast of hand-crafted terracotta and ceramic tiles, of rich *alcobaça* fabrics and carefully chosen (often naïve) paintings. We loved the Chapel room (one of two 'specials') with its high ceilings and bathroom sitting snugly inside what once was a chimney breast. Lounge and bar are just as special and entirely candlelit at night. Such a peaceful place, and Isabel a delight. *Minimum stay 2-4 nights depending on season.*

rooms	7: 6 doubles/twins, 1 suite.
price	€ 100-€ 185; suite € 205-€ 240; single € 80.
meals	Dinner € 20, on request.
closed	Rarely.
directions	From Faro, N125 then IP1 for Spain. Exit 7 to Tavira; under archway, over r'bout & T-junc., right after church, following signs 'Centro Saude'. Right past army barracks, then 1st left. After 200m, fork right to Convento.

Isabel Maria Castanho Paes
tel	+351 281 321573
fax	+351 281 325632

map 6   entry 143

Quinta da Fonte Bispo

Estrada National 270, Fonte do Bispo, 8800-161 Tavira, Faro

The benign climate, exceptional vegetation, closeness to the sea and interesting folk architecture mean that the gentle hills of the Algarve hinterland remain a good choice for a holiday. This old farmstead will draw you deep into an affection for the region; we can see why painting courses are held here. It is a long, low, white building with pretty chimney stacks and broad bands of blue around doors and windows – typical of the area. Parts of the farm are 200 years old but it has been completely renovated. The six apartments in the converted outbuildings of the farm, fronting a cobbled central patio, were designed with families in mind: open-plan sitting rooms have beds which double up as sofas and there is a small kitchenette. The style is local and 'country': herringbone terracotta floor, beamed and bamboo roof, simple yet adequate shower rooms. There is a large communal sitting room in similar style but most of the year you will be out by the pool; find a shady spot beneath the orange, almond or olive trees. The restaurant serves Mediterranean and Portuguese food, and you can also enjoy a sauna, table-tennis, pool and mini-gym.

rooms	6 self-catering apartments.
price	€65–€92 for 2. Call for further details of prices.
meals	Lunch €15; dinner €20.
closed	Rarely.
directions	From Faro, IP1 for Spain. Pass Loulé then exit for Santa Catarina. There, right for Tavira. Quinta signed on left after 1km.

Helena Brito Neto

tel	+351 281 971484
fax	+351 281 971484
e-mail	info@qtfontebispo.com
web	www.qtfontebispo.com

WHAT'S IN THE BACK OF THE BOOK? ...

USEFUL VOCABULARY

Basic food				
	Acepipes / entrados	Hors d'oeuvres	*Arroz*	Rice
	Azeitonas	Olives	*Manteiga*	Butter
	Ovos	Eggs	*Pão*	Bread
	Pimenta	Pepper	*Sal*	Salt
	Salada	Salad	*Queijo*	Cheese

In restaurants				
	Almoço	Lunch	*Colher*	Spoon
	Conta	The bill	*Copo*	Glass
	Ementa	Menu	*Faca*	Knife
	Garfo	Fork	*Garrafa*	Bottle
	Jantar	Dinner	*Pequeno almoço*	Breakfast

Meat, Poultry & Game				
	Borrego	Lamb	*Cabrito*	Kid
	Carne de porco	Pork	*Carneiro*	Mutton
	Coelho	Rabbit	*Dobrada*	Tripe
	Galinha	Chicken	*Morcela*	Blood pudding
	Pato	Duck	*Perú*	Turkey
	Salsicha	Sausage	*Vitela*	Veal

Fish & Shellfish				
	Ameijoas	Clams	*Anchovas*	Anchovies
	Atum	Tuna	*Camarões*	Shrimp
	Caranguejo	Crab	*Gambas*	Prawns
	Lagosta	Lobster	*Lulas*	Squid
	Mexilhões	Mussels	*Ostras*	Oysters
	Polvo	Octopus	*Salmão*	Salmon
	Sardinhas	Sardines	*Truta*	Trout

Vegetables				
	Alcachofra	Artichoke	*Alface*	Lettuce
	Alho	Garlic	*Batatas*	Potatoes
	Cebola	Onion	*Cenoura*	Carrot
	Cogumelos	Mushrooms	*Ervilhas*	Peas
	Espargos	Asparagus	*Espinafre*	Spinach
	Favas	Broad beans	*Pepino*	Cucumber

Specialities		
	Açorda (de marisco)	Bread-based stew (cooked with spices and shellfish)
	Arroz de marisco	Seafood paella
	Bife à Portuguesa	Beef steak, topped with mustard sauce & fried egg
	Cataplanas	Stew of fish, clams and ham or sausage
	Espeteda mista	Mixed meat kebab
	Frango no churrasco	Barbecued chicken
	Leitão assado	Roast suckling pig

USEFUL VOCABULARY

Before arriving (over the telephone)	Do you have a room for the night?	*Tem um quarto para esta noite?*
	How much does it cost?	*Quanto custa?*
	We'll be arriving at about 7pm.	*Nós chegaremos por volta das sete da tarde.*
	We're lost!	*Estamos perdidos!*
	We'll be arriving late.	*Vamos chegar tarde.*
	I'm in the phone box at…	*Estou na cabine telefónica em…*
	I'm in the 'Oporto' bar in…	*Estou no bar 'Oporto' em…*
	Do you have any animals?	*Você tem algum animal?*
	I'm allergic to cats.	*Sou alérgico a gatos.*
	We would like to have dinner.	*Queríamos jantar.*
On arrival	Hello! I'm Mr/Mrs X.	*Olá! eu sou o Senhor/Senhora X.*
	We found your name in this book.	*Encontramos o seu nome neste livro.*
	Where can we leave the car?	*Onde podemos deixar o carro?*
	Could you help us with our bags?	*Podia ajudar-nos com as nossas malas?*
	Could I leave this picnic food in your fridge?	*Podia deixar estas garrafas para picnic no seu frigorífico?*
	Could I heat up the baby's bottle?	*Podia aquecer o biberon?*
	How much will you charge for that?	*Quanto é que você cobrará por isto?*
Things that you need/that go wrong	Do you have an extra pillow/blanket?	*Você tem uma outra almofada/um outro cobertor?*
	A light bulb needs replacing.	*É preciso mudar uma lâmpada.*
	The heating isn't on.	*O aquecedor não está ligado.*
	We've a problem with the plumbing.	*Temos um problema com a canalização.*
	How does the air conditioning work?	*Como funciona o ar condicionado?*
	Do you have a quieter room?	*Tem um quarto menos barulhento?*
	Where can I hang these wet clothes?	*Onde posso secar estas roupas?*
	Could we have some soap?	*Queríamos sabonete por favor?*
	Could you turn the volume down?	*Pode baixar o volume?*
	Please could you give us some hot water to make tea – we have our own tea bags!	*Podia nos dar água quente para o nosso chá – temos as nossas próprias saquetas de chá.*
How the house/hotel works	When do you begin serving breakfast?	*A que horas começa a servir o pequeno almoço?*
	We'd like to order some drinks.	*Queríamos tomar algumas bebidas, por favor.*
	Can the children play in the garden?	*As crianças podem brincar no jardim?*
	Is there any danger?	*É perigoso?*
	Can we leave the children with you?	*Podemos deixar as crianças convosco?*

USEFUL VOCABULARY

Local information	Where can we buy petrol?	*Onde fica a próxima estação de serviço?*
	How far is the nearest shop?	*Fica muito longe a próxima loja?*
	We need a doctor.	*Precisamos dum médico.*
	Where is the chemist's?	*Onde há uma farmácia?*
	Where is the police station?	*Onde fica o posto de polícia?*
	Where's a good place to eat?	*Onde há um sítio onde se coma bem?*
	Where can we find a cash-dispenser?	*Onde há uma caixa automática?*
	Do you know of any local festivities?	*Sabe de algumas festividades locais?*
On leaving	What time must we leave the room?	*A que horas temos de libertar/deixar o quarto?*
	We'd like to pay the bill.	*Queríamos pagar a conta.*
	How much do I owe you?	*Quanto devo?*
	We hope to be back.	*Esperamos regressar.*
	We've had a very pleasant stay.	*Tivemos uma estadia muito agradável.*
	This is a beautiful spot.	*Este é um lugar muito bonito.*
	Thank you so much.	*Muito obrigado/a.*

Eating out (or in)	Where's there a good bar?	*Onde há um bom bar?*
	Could we eat outside, please?	*Podemos comer lá fora?*
	What's today's set menu?	*Qual é o menu para hoje?*
	What do you recommend?	*O que nos recomenda?*
	What vegetarian dishes do you have?	*Que pratos vegetarianos tem?*
	Do you have a wine list?	*Tem uma lista de vinhos?*
	This food is cold!	*Esta comida está fria.*
	Do you have some salt please?	*Tem sal por favor?*
	What tapas do you have?	*Que aperitivos tem?*
	A plate of this one.	*Uma dose deste.*
	Please keep the change.	*Guarde o troco.*
	Where are the toilets?	*Onde ficam as casas de banho?*
	The toilet is locked.	*As casas de banho estão fechadas.*
	It was a delicious meal.	*Foi uma óptima refeição.*
	I'd like a white coffee.	*Queria um café com leite*
	black coffee	*café simples*
	weaker coffee	*café fraco*
	coffee with just a little milk	*café com um pouco de leite*
	tea**	*chá*
	camomile tea	*chá de camomila*

**remember, the safest way to order tea with milk is to ask for *um chá e um pouco de leite, mas aparte*. It's tempting to ask for *chá com leite* – but you may well end up with a glass of hot milk with a teabag plonked on the top! Milk is nearly always UHT so if you really need your tea we recommend drinking it with a slice of lemon *chá com limão*. Or take your own along and just ask for *jarro com água quente* in the bar. Your request will rarely be refused.

ABOUT EATING IN PORTUGAL &
A SMATTERING OF RECIPES

Carol Dymond, our chief inspector in Portugal, has lived there for years, is passionate about good food, loves to cook and has recently been working as chef at the Quinta do Barranco da Estrada (entry number 121). We invited her to contribute some thoughts on Portuguese food, eating 'out' and 'in', and some of her recipes... here they are.

Restaurant food in Portugal can be quite limited. It tends to be simply cooked, relying on the intrinsic quality of the ingredients – meat, generally (pork, especially in the Alentejo, is very tasty), lots of chips, and rarely a vegetable in sight!

In many of the manor houses, hotels and *quintas* you will get a better taste of real Portuguese. Your hosts may well treat you to wonderful local specialities and classic regional dishes; one may feed you fresh trout from their own farm, another home-grown lamb. You will probably be treated to delicious biscuits and cakes by your hosts – after which I doubt you will manage to keep out of the *pasteleria* for the rest of your visit!

What I am aiming for when I cook at the Quinta is to give the guests a taste of good Portuguese home cooking, along with the more international dishes they expect. My personal style leans towards a fusion of wholefood, vegetarian, even vegan food, with influences from the middle and far East, as well as the Mediterranean. Combining this with traditional Portuguese cooking is something of a challenge, as anyone who has eaten in a normal restaurant here will appreciate.

Entradas – starters

In simple restaurants – along with the olives, small tins of sardine paste and ersatz cheese spread – you may be lucky and get an interesting little salad, maybe one of tuna and black-eyed beans, or the scary-sounding *salada de orelha* ('salad of the ear'), or more often a small wholecheese. This could be a fresh goat's cheese, mild and moist, or a harder, dryer one, most likely a sheep's cheese.

A neighbour of mine, Edite, used to make wonderful goat's cheese at home (that has all stopped now, due to EEC regulations: sad, I feel) and I enjoyed the fresh ones as an ingredient in many dishes, from salad with tomato and basil (or avocado) to cheesecake. She put salt on the cheeses, and left them to dry for a few days, when they would be stored in oil, or left to get hard enough to grate, in place of parmesan. When they were just hard enough to slice easily, I used them to make this recipe.

ABOUT EATING IN PORTUGAL & A SMATTERING OF RECIPES

Lulu's Starter

(Lulu is the owner of Quinta do Barranco do Estrada.)

Marinade the sliced cheese along with slices of skinned cucumber in a vinaigrette dressing, and garnish with capers, black olives and finely chopped mint. Serve well chilled.

I was told, when visiting a manor house in the north of Portugal, that they serve sheep's cheese with *Marmelada*, a solid quince jam, which can be cut in slices, and that this combination is called *Romeo and Juliet*. As they say, *Marmelada com queijo, sabe do beijo* ('Marmelada with cheese tastes like a kiss').

The word *Marmelada* comes from *Marmelo*, meaning quince, and is the origin of our word 'marmalade' – originally made from quince rather than oranges. Now oranges were once known as *portucale*, before Portugal existed, so is marmalade named after a fruit it is not made from, and Portugal named after oranges? Maybe you can enlighten me!

Sopa – Soup

Soup is often the only way to get your vegetables in a restaurant; it's almost always good. Even in the most humble café you are unlikely to be given something from a packet or tin. The usual method for making vegetable soup is the one I have always used: brought up on Elizabeth David I limit the number of different vegetables so that one or two dominate.

Basic Method

Fry onions and garlic gently in olive oil (I use butter, too, though a Portuguese cook wouldn't) then add the vegetables, and 'sweat' them over low heat with the lid on for 10 minutes or so, to bring out the flavours. Add water or stock, salt and pepper and any herbs and spices the individual recipe requires, and cook until the vegetables are soft. Whizz in a blender and adjust seasoning.

My 'splendid blended' soups: a couple of recommendations…

Carrot and Coriander

Lots of carrots, a couple of potatoes or sweet potatoes, ground coriander, finished with chopped fresh coriander. (I never let fresh coriander cook – it can give a metallic taste – but add it just before serving.)

Pumpkin

These are grown a lot, used to thicken soup, to make into a sweet filling for cakes, and to fatten up pigs in winter, and you often see them stored on the roof, or around the well, up out of the wet, where they will keep for months, looking decorative. I make this soup to cheer the cooler winter days.

As above, with a generous amount of garlic, adding cinnamon, cumin, paprika and a little chilli and nutmeg. Add a little tomato purée, or, even better, 'massa de pimentão' (a purée of sweet red peppers available in jars and a most useful ingredient) to adjust the colour and flavour, but don't overdo it. Finish off with a touch of green — chopped marjoram, coriander or parsley.

Here is a soup commonly served in restaurants…

Caldo Verde

Use the basic method, but with only onion, garlic and potato; then add very finely sliced kale or dark green cabbage. (Market stalls often have a machine which does this for you, and you can also buy it in supermarkets.) Cook until the kale is tender, and serve with a slice of 'chouriço' sausage in each bowl.

Açorda à Alentejana

This is real peasant food; my elderly neighbours almost lived on this — a meal in itself.

Mash fresh coriander with garlic and coarse salt in a pestle and mortar. Put in your soup bowl and add a generous amount of good olive oil and some torn-up dry white bread. This should be the sourdough bread for which the Alentejo is well known, but any dense bread will do. Meanwhile, poach an egg, and pour it, water and all, into the bowl. Variations include tomato or grilled green pepper or 'bacalhão'; sometimes even the water the fish was cooked in is used to poach the egg. There's resourcefulness for you!

Gaspacho à Alentejana

Really, a summer version of the recipe above. A guest at the Quinta said it was the best gazpacho he had ever had, so I'll give you the recipe I used, with quantities for four.

Mash 3 cloves of garlic with a tablespoonful of salt, and put into a tureen. Add 3 tablespoonfuls of olive oil, 4 of vinegar, and some oregano. Blend a tin of tomatoes (or half a dozen very ripe skinned fresh ones) to a purée, and add. Cut up half of a cucumber, a tomato and a green pepper into small dice, and add. Pour in 1.5 litres of iced water and 200g of diced dry bread and serve at once. I use fried croutons as they don't disintegrate so fast, and I add finely chopped coriander or parsley.

Main courses
Peixe – Fish

Grilled fish, one of the delights of Portugal, is usually served with plain boiled potatoes and a tiny salad. Sardines are left unadorned, and usually un-gutted, but larger fish like bass or bream are sometimes scattered with raw garlic and chopped coriander. With luck, you will be eating the fish gazing onto the very sea where it swam hours before landing on your plate.

ABOUT EATING IN PORTUGAL & A SMATTERING OF RECIPES

Two favourite fish dishes…

Arroz de Marisco

The Portuguese version of paella, but just seafood, no meat, and more liquid; crammed with lobster, and crab, it is served in the deep pan in which it is cooked: incredibly messy to eat (they always supply lots of napkins) but delicious, and good fun to share…

Caldeirada

There are many versions of this mixed fish stew, with strict rules about which fish to use, but it seems the important thing is that they have a firm flesh which does not fall apart. In markets here you can usually get the special mixture. I have even made it with frozen hake (shock horror!) but it was still good, and had no bones.

Simply layer thinly sliced potatoes, onion, green pepper and tomato with your fish in a deep pan, sprinkling a little paprika, salt, pepper and chopped parsley between the layers. Slip a bay leaf in somewhere. Pour over a generous amount of olive oil, add a bottle of dry white wine (top up with a little water if you need to) and cook on the stove without stirring, until the potato is well cooked, but the fish hasn't totally disintegrated. Serve straight from the pot.

Bacalhão

Most famous of all Portuguese food must be *bacalhão*, the dried salt cod fishermen have been bringing back from the North Sea for centuries. (A good read: Mark Kulansky's book *Cod.*) It is a bit of an aquired taste, but I have here one of the most accessible of the 365 recipes. *Bacalhão* is most often served plain and simple, as in this unlikely-sounding but wonderful combination…

Bacalhão à Brás (for four)

400g bacalhão, 3 tablespoons olive oil, 500g potatoes, 6 eggs, 3 onions, 1 clove garlic.

The cod is soaked overnight, then shredded. Onions are fried, along with the garlic, in olive oil. Very fine potato chips are fried and drained (in Portugal, they also sell these in packets, like crisps). Then the fish is added to the onion, to absorb some of the oil as it cooks. The potato chips are added, then beaten eggs, seasoned with salt and pepper, cooked for a few minutes and served sprinkled with parsley and black olives.

Bacalhão fish cakes are good served with sauce.

Chilli Sauce

Roast in a dry pan cumin seeds, chillies or chilli powder (you can get an African one called 'jindungo' which is very good), cinnamon and a little aniseed. Add olive oil, garlic and finely chopped onion and cook gently till transparent. Add tomatoes (skinned fresh ones, or tinned) and whatever you can lay your hands on, or improvise, in the way of 'massa de pimentão' — red pepper paste. Add some tomato purée, reduce by cooking gently for 20-30 minutes, and then whizz it all to a smooth texture, adding salt if necessary, black pepper, a little sugar to balance the acidity of the tomatoes, and a couple of squares of bitter chocolate to enrichen the sauce (a Mexican trick!).

I don't put quantities because it doesn't really matter, so much depends on the quality of the ingredients, and your taste.

Falafel

Not remotely Portuguese, but chickpeas are widely grown and used here, and the spices are commonly used — thanks to centuries of Moorish occupation.

Soak chickpeas overnight, drain and put into a food processor with some garlic, powdered cumin, paprika, coriander and a little chilli. Add chopped fresh parsley, coriander and one teaspoonful of bicarbonate of soda for each kilo of chickpeas. This helps to keep them light, but don't overdo it or they will explode! Add as much salt and black pepper as your taste dictates; I usually fry a little of the mix to test the flavour before forming the mix into walnut sized balls. (I squash them a bit, to elongate them, so they cook evenly.) Deep fry in hot oil, and serve with the spicy sauce as well as a yogurt, mint and lemon juice. Good with a leafy green salad and tabbouleh.

Carne – Meat

When I first arrived in Portugal, I chose from one of those hilariously translated menus which helpfully described *Cozido à Portuguesa* as 'boiled Portuguese'. When it was put, steaming, in front of me, I thought for a moment that the translation had been accurate after all: unspeakable bits of body, gristly knuckles and slimy sausage sat among boiled potato, carrot and cabbage. I felt a bit better when I recognised a snout!
(I was a vegetarian for quite a while after that.)

Also worth knowing: *Cabidela* is a chicken stew, whose sauce is made with red wine and blood, and *Sarrabulho* is a pork offal stew — neither are for the squeamish.

Highly recommended, on the other hand, are the following:

Carne de Porco Alentejana, a pork dish with clams, and *Ensopado de Borrego* or *Ensopada de Cabrito*, a rich stew of lamb or kid, usually with a slice of fried bread underneath to soak up the sauce.
Chanfana is a goat stew, cooked in a special black clay dish.
Frango na Púcara, a chicken casserole, is also named after the dish it is cooked and served in.

ABOUT EATING IN PORTUGAL & A SMATTERING OF RECIPES

By the way, 'Bife' does not mean beef, but simply a thin piece of meat.

My meat recipe does not try to be too authentic (the Portuguese do that so well) but uses ingredients which are commonly found here.

Carol's Mexican Turkey Rolls

Beat 6-8 turkey breast steaks with a meat hammer till very thin.
Lay a slice of 'presunto' (thinly sliced smoked ham) on top of each one.
In a food processor, make a stuffing from the following ingredients:

100g each of breadcrumbs, pine nuts, almonds, raisins; 1 onion, chopped;
3 cloves of garlic, crushed; salt, pepper, paprika, chilli, coriander and
cinnamon to taste; 1 egg.

Roll out into sausage shapes, almost the width of the meat, place on top,
and roll up, tucking in any untidy edges. Place on an oiled oven tray, with
the join underneath, brush with oil and bake for 30-40 minutes (covered in
foil to start with, but let them brown a bit at the end). Serve with the chilli
sauce poured over, and a sprinkling of sesame seeds and fresh coriander.
Vegetarians can have the stuffing 'sausage' without the meat around it.
These are also very good and rather decorative cut into slices when cold.

I serve these with baked potatoes, accompanied by sour cream, guacamole, and my spicy relish, which goes something like this.

Pumpkin and Tomato Chutney

Put 1kg each of pumpkin, tomato, onion chopped roughly, and 1kg sugar,
preferably brown, in a preserving pan, along with most of a head of garlic,
2 tablespoonfuls of salt, 2 teaspoonfuls each of ground ginger, paprika, black
pepper, allspice, 1 teaspoonful of chilli and 1 litre of vinegar. Cook slowly
for an hour or so, until it becomes jam-like; stir to prevent itsticking. Once
there is no free liquid on the top, remove from heat and put into hot, clean
jars, with vinegar-proof lids. Keep for at least 3 months,to allow to mellow.

There are thousands of fantastic sweets, puddings and pastries in Portugal; many originally came from the convents, so have names like *Barriga da Freira* (Nun's Belly), *Pasteis de Santa Clara* or even *Orelhas da Abade*: oh dear, ears again, the Abbot's this time. Many desserts are very eggy and very sweet.

Sobremesas – Puddings

Pudim Flan is my favourite, a rather solid version of crème caramel. *Molotoff* is made out of all the egg whites left over from the above – a cloud of soft, sweet, caramel-topped meringue. *Arroz Doce* is a very good cold rice pudding with lemon rind and egg yolk added, and cinnamon sprinkled in a pattern on the top.

I have a variation on *Mousse de Chocolate* – it has no eggs but is just as rich, and the touch of orange gives it a Portuguese flavour.

ABOUT EATING IN PORTUGAL & A SMATTERING OF RECIPES

Chocolate Pots

Shave the peel from an orange. Boil 300ml cream with the peel. Remove from heat while you grate or chop 175g dark chocolate. Fish the peel from the cream, bring cream back to the boil, remove from heat, and whisk in the chocolate. Add a tablespoonful of orange-flavoured alcohol (brandy, cointreau or triple sec). Pour into 4 little ramekins, and leave to set in the fridge. Decorate with a piece of crystallised orange peel.

You may also be offered something called *Baba de Camelo*, which I am told means 'camel's spit'. Its chief ingredient, happily, is condensed milk.

Pasteis de Nata

Better by far are these are those lovely little custard tarts that you can buy in every *pasteleria* in Portugal: I have had several goes at perfecting these, and even the failures have been scrummy.

Roll out puff pastry (I use frozen) to a rectangle 20cm long and 0.5cm thick. Dampen the top slightly to be sure it sticks together, and roll up, lengthways. Cut it up with a very sharp knife into 1cm wide slices. You should now have discs of spiralled pastry, which you have to persuade into lightly buttered, deep patty tins. Put your thumb into the middle of the spiral, pressing gently with your fingers on the outside, to form a shallow bowl. Place in tin. With damp fingers, pinch the pastry up the sides of the tins, so it's thin, but without holes. (This is just like making a pinch pot in clay and reminds me of when I was a pottery teacher back in the 70s. It is also much easier than it sounds, and is necessary in order to get the spiral construction right: you will see what I mean when you eat one.)

In a double boiler make a custard with half a litre of cream, 200g sugar (that you have stored, ideally, with a vanilla pod), 2 teaspoonfuls of flour and a little grated lemon rind. Take off the heat when it starts to thicken, and cool till tepid before adding 6 egg yolks. Then pour into pastry cases. Bake in a very hot oven for about 15 minutes. The filling will rise, and then sink when cool. They should be a bit burnt on the top; if not, finish off with a blowtorch, as one would Crème Brûlée. The finishing touch is to sprinkle icing sugar and cinnamon on, just before you eat them.

As I write, someone is eating the first of the latest batch. "Absolutely divine!", he says.

Do send me feedback on foodie experiences good and bad. I would like to do a food book, and your comments would be very helpful.

Carol Dymond

WINE

Legend has it that the Phoenicians brought the vine to Portugal, but it was the Romans who developed viniculture. They were followed by the Swabians, Visigoths and Moors, and despite the Koran's injunctions against *al-cohol* (an Arab word meaning 'the spirit') the Portuguese continued to make wine. Today, most vineyards are owned by farmers with smallholdings who sell their grapes to the local cooperatives. *Vinho tinto* (red), *branco* (white), *verde* (green) and *rosa* are great value, and when eating out, don't overlook the *vinho da casa* (house wine) – it will probably be excellent; for a few pounds the most discerning palate will be delighted by *a reserva*.

The main wine-producing areas:

Alentejo A large, southern area whose wines are among the best. Try the Redondo, Reguengos and Borba reds.

Algarve The reds, excellent with food, are light ruby. The dry whites make fine aperitifs.

Bairrada A rich, enduring flavour. Look for São João, Aliança, São Domingos, Império and Barroção.

Colares On the Atlantic coast the vines flourish between cane windbreaks. The reds are full of aromatic fruit and in time have a velvety taste.

Dão Most wine from these hilly terraces is red, with strong colour and a taste with real bite. Try São João, Grão Vasco, Acácio, Rittos and Caves Velhas.

Douro This northern valley was originally demarcated only for port, but now over half the grapes are for light wines. Try Barca Velha, Penajora, Champalimaud and Acácio.

Port wines Only made in the Douro. When enough sugar has been converted into alcohol, fermentation is stopped by adding the wine to grape brandy in a ratio of 4:1. Maturation varies and port wine ranges from 19-22 degrees for red and 16.5-20 for white.

WINE

Oeste This region produces excellent reds including the rather dry, cedary flavours from Óbidos, the softer Alenquer and the gutsy Arruda reds.

Ribatejo Here the vine flourishes in poor soil, but also in the rich flood plains of the Tagus. Reds are deep in colour, with a fruity taste and aftertaste. Sample Caves Velhas Romeira, Teobar of Dom Teodósio, Almeiria and Torre Velha.

Vinho Verde This means 'green wine', but the colour is pale yellow. The name is given because of the wine's young taste and because the extreme north, where the vines grow, has more rain and greener countryside. Rather than the usual uniform rows, the vines ramble freely over hedges, houses and pergolas. *Vinho verdes* are light and perfect with seafood. Try Alvarinho, João Pires, Gatão, Lagosta, Solar das Boucas and Palácio de Brejoeira.

FADO

The lights are low and two players are crouched over their instruments, one the pear-shaped *guitarra* with 12 metal strings, the other the gut-strung guitar. They begin playing a plaintive, passionate melody and then a woman steps forward. Her head is thrown back, her eyes are half closed, and she sings of love in the simple, open-throated manner dictated by long tradition. Against the simple rhythm and silvery lines of the *guitarra* she sings as freely as a jazz player, and the push and pull of her melodic improvisation, the ornamental flourishes and emotional intensity, command complete attention from the audience.

This is Portuguese *fado*, and the word, from the Latin *fatum,* means 'fate'. These songs of fate and destiny have come from the backstreets, but *fado's* origins are older, in Brazil and Africa, in songs brought home by sailors and heard in quayside taverns. The songs, sung by men and women, are about the myriad variations on the themes of love, broken hearts and *saudades*, the yearnings of the soul, and about the old quarters of Lisbon, such as Mouraria, Alfama and Bairro Alto.

Probably the greatest *fado* singer of them all was Amália Rodrigues (1921-1999). She began as a fruit seller in the streets of Lisbon, singing for pleasure, and rose to become an international star and a Portuguese icon. She said: "The *fado* is a song of the soul, a kind of cry. In Portugal, when something sad happens, you say 'It was my *fado*'. It's a music which touches people all over the world. The *fado* is very simple, with almost no harmony or melody. You could say that they're poor songs, and that you have to be rich inside to sing *fado* well. I can't rehearse a *fado* and sing it one way tonight and the same way tomorrow. I don't know how to do that. I sing from the heart, without process or techniques, with nothing but me and my voice." Today you can judge her genius for yourself, for numerous recordings by Amália are available. The finest *fadistas* today are probably Cristina Branco, who has a superb and original voice, and Carlos Zel (men also sing *fado*); also worth hearing are Dulce Pontes, Mafalda Arnaud and Mízia, singer of 'new fado'.

The *guitarra* players are usually virtuosos who provide counter-melodies to the singers' line and also play instrumentals. One of the greatest was the late Carlos Paredes; others are António Chainho and Luisa Amaro, of the Trio de Guitarras.

FADO

One of Portugal's finest and most original groups is undoubtedly Madredeus, featuring the wonderful voice of Teresa Salgueiro; this ensemble, of acoustic guitars, cello and accordion, makes hauntingly beautiful music, truly Portuguese in character, and has achieved international success. Listen to Antologia and O Paraíso. Another original is Rão Kyao (flute and sax); his Fado Bailado is a classic of *fado* melodies.

Although Portugal is considered Latin, many of its roots lie in Celtic culture. The rich and beautiful melodies of the folk music have been beautifully played for years by the Brigada Vitor Jara group. Traditional folk is also the domain of the group *Gaiteiros de Lisboa*. Folk diversity and some of Portugal's finest voices can be heard on the album *Cantigas de Amigos*, by João Balão & José Moz Carrapa.

In the jazz realm, Portugal's finest and most original players include Carlos Martins' *Orquestre Sons da Lusofonia*, António Pinho Vargas (sax & piano), Laurent Philipe (trumpet), the quintets and trios led by Bernardo Moreira (double bass), and the Carlos Barreto Trio.

If you can hear performances by classical pianists Maria Jõao Pires, António Rosado, Pedro Burmester or Artur Pizarro, all of whom have recorded, take the opportunity.

Portugal has many annual music festivals of classical, choral, folk, jazz and rock. Recorded music is good value and the choice is wide, including the delights of Brazil.
Happy hunting and listening.

EXPLORING PORTUGAL

Not much is known of Portugal beyond the famous Algarve, yet this little country has an amazingly varied landscape. Stray off the well-trodden track and discover its hidden corners: the lush green Minho of the north where vinho verde is produced; the deserted beaches of the Costa Verde; the wild Atlantic beaches of the Alentejo; the faded charm of the old capital Coimbra; the Moorish and Roman grandeur of the south. And the Natural Parks of Portugal - established some thirty years ago to protect threatened species of flora, fauna, fish and fowl.

Portugal's first Natural Park (1971) is the wild and beautiful Peneda-Gerês to the north. It is one of the last refuges of the Royal Eagle and the wolf – and offers remote and challenging walking for the adventurous. More wolves in the Montesinho Park in Trás-os-Montes, whose immense black oak and sweet chestnut forests are also alive with roe deer, fox, wild cat, badger, otter and birds of prey.

Travel south and you reach the massive Serra da Estrela, whose network of trails makes this exciting – and challenging - hiking country. On the lower slopes black oaks give way to juniper while on the uppermost pastures rare gentian thrive. Sheep and goats roam the hills; the country's most famous cheese comes from here, creamy, pungent Queijo da Serra.

On the Lisbon coast is the verdant Sintra-Cascais Natural Park, home to the tourist towns of Cascais and Sintra. In the 18th century the stunning 'Mountain of the Moon' became the summer place of residence for the nobility of Lisbon, so visit the historic hillside town of Sintra, and out of season if you can. The Roca Cape is the most westerly point of the continent of Europe, and to the south lies the biggest expanse of sands and dunes on the continent.

Down to the Extremadura and the Natural Reserve of the Tejo Estuary. Its colony of avocets alone makes this reserve one of major importance: half the European population of this species lives among the marshes and salt pans. And the lush, mild Arrábida Natural Park a fraction further south, is a source of joy to geologists and biologists alike, thanks to its fossilized layers of limestone and sand, its 70 species of seaweed, 300 species of butterfly and 450 of beetle.

EXPLORING PORTUGAL

More marshes, rushes and dunes in the Sado Estuary Reserve, where ecotourism thrives. Go flamingo-, stork- or dolphin-watching by boat with trained monitors. This area also teems with swans, herons, ducks, otters and turtles.

East of Faro, on Portugal's southern tip is the Ria Formosa, one of the most important wetlands in Europe and a wintering ground for migrating birds. It's home too to the rare and exotic Sultan chicken, whose numbers at the last count totalled 20. Take time to explore the gentle hills of the Algarve hinterland and its fascinating old towns - the 37 tiled churches of elegant Tavira, Olhao with its cobbled streets and Moorish terraces, and the old Arab principality that gave rise to Faro.

Portugal is a birdwatcher's paradise. The best time for birds is from mid March to mid June, particularly in the Alentejo. Here habitats range from vast areas of oak forest to precipitous rocky outcrops to the open steppes of Castro Verde; on a good day keen watchers may note up to 60 species… bustards, kites, shrikes, warblers, storks, swallows, Blue Rock Thrushes, Spanish Imperial Eagles – all the world's species, it seems, congregate here, and each year more and more White Storks 'forget' to migrate to Africa and can be seen the whole year round.

Source material: www.portugalvirtual.pt

WORLD HERITAGE SITES

Porto (Oporto)
Thriving port and commercial city in medieval times, in a lovely setting at the mouth of the river Duoro. Visit the 12th-century cathedral with original Romanesque rose windows and elegant Georgian cloister, the opulent neoclassical Palácio da Bolsa (1842) and the Barredo quarter with its steep cobbled streets.

Alto Douro
Grapes love the area's hot dry climate and rocky soil: there's a long history of viticulture in the Douro, particularly of port. Hotel boats for tourists have replaced the Rabelo boats that used to transport wine down the fast-flowing river to the markets of the world.

Côa Valley
Rock art from the Upper Paleolithic Age to the 17th-century along the Côa River's last 17km course. See ancient drawings of mountain goats, horses, deer and some rare engravings of fish; fine Iron Age engravings of warriors; religious and profane motifs.

Mosteiro da Alcoba
100km north of Lisbon, begun in 1178, an entire group of exceptionally preserved medieval buildings and church.

Mosteiro de Batalha
A glorious Gothic monument, spectacular when flood-lit at night.

The Convent of Christ in Tomar
Built on a hill overlooking the city in three distinct walled enclosures, the Templar Castle and Convent of the Knights of Christ is the principle monument in Tomar.

Torre de Belem
Resembling a tower of icing on a wedding cake, the exquisitely carved monument was built 1514-1520 as an essential part of the defensive system for the mouth of the Tajo. It is one of the world's most beautiful examples of military architecture.

Mosteiro dos Jerónimos
Small but magical chapel commissioned by Prince Henry the Navigator in Belem in 1502, and built in the unique Manueline style. Belem was a 16th-century port (no longer in existence) from which ships set sail on their voyages of discovery in Portugal's heyday.

Sintra
Fabulous walled hillside city containing a rich collection of monuments from different ages, dominated by the astonishing Palácio Nacional. It also benefits from a naturally dense vegetation, beautiful romantic parks, a wonderful climate and a vibrant musical culture.

Évora
The capital city of the Alentejo, a lovely city of pastel-painted facades, whose narrow streets evoke memories of a Moorish presence. It has a grand past and was chosen by several kings to serve as headquarters for their court.

Guimarães
Exceptionally well-preserved example of the evolution of a medieval settlement into a modern township.

WHAT IS ALASTAIR SAWDAY PUBLISHING?

Twenty or so of us work in converted barns on a farm near Bristol, close enough to the city for a bicycle ride and far enough for a silence broken only by horses and the occasional passage of a tractor. Some editors work in the countries they write about, e.g. France; others work from the UK but are based outside the office. We enjoy each other's company, celebrate every event possible, and work in an easy-going but committed environment.

These books owe their style and mood to Alastair's miscellaneous career and his interest in the community and the environment. He has taught overseas, worked with refugees, run development projects abroad, founded a travel company and several environmental organisations. There has been a slightly mad streak evident throughout, not least in his driving of a waste-paper-collection lorry for a year, the manning of stalls at jumble sales and the pursuit of causes long before they were considered sane.

Back to the travel company: trying to take his clients to eat and sleep in places that were not owned by corporations and assorted bandits he found dozens of very special places in France – farms, châteaux etc – a list that grew into the first book, *French Bed and Breakfast*. It was a celebration of 'real' places to stay and the remarkable people who run them.

The publishing company grew from that first and rather whimsical French book. It started as a mild crusade, and there it stays – full of 'attitude', and the more appealing for it. For we still celebrate the unusual, the beautiful, the individual. We are passionate about rejecting the banal, the ugly, the pompous and the indifferent and we are passionate too about 'real' food. Alastair is a trustee of the Soil Association and keen to promote organic growing and consuming by owners and visitors.

It is a source of deep pleasure to us to know that there are many thousands of people who share our views. We are by no means alone in trumpeting the virtues of resisting the destruction and uniformity of so much of our culture – and the cultures of other nations, too.

We run a company in which people and values matter. We love to hear of new friendships between those in the book and those using it, and to know that there are many people – among them farmers – who have been enabled to pursue their decent lives thanks to the extra income our books bring them.

ALASTAIR SAWDAY'S

**British Hotels,
Inns & Other Places**
Edition 4   £12.99

British Bed & Breakfast
Edition 7   £14.99

British Holiday Homes
Edition 1   £9.99

**Bed & Breakfast for
Garden Lovers**
Edition 2   £14.99

French Bed & Breakfast
Edition 8   £15.99

Paris Hotels
Edition 4   £9.99

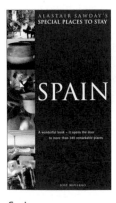

Spain
Edition 5   £13.99

Ireland
Edition 4   £12.99

Portugal
Edition 2   £9.99

**French Hotels, Inns &
Other Places**
Edition 2   £11.95

Italy
Edition 2   £11.95

French Holiday Homes
Edition 1   £11.99

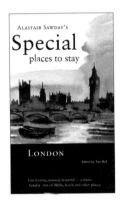

London
Edition 1   £9.99

THE LITTLE EARTH BOOK

The Little Earth Book
James Bruges

'Only dead fish float with the current;
live fish swim against it'.

3rd Edition

Over 30,000 copies sold.

A fascinating read. The earth is now desperately vulnerable; so are we. Original, stimulating short essays about what is going wrong with our planet, and about the greatest challenge of our century: how to save the Earth for us all. It is succinct, yet intellectually credible, well-referenced, wry yet deadly serious.

Researched and written by a Bristol architect, James Bruges, The Little Earth Book is a clarion call to action, a stimulating collection of short essays on today's most important environmental concerns, from global warming and poisoned food to unfettered economic growth, Third World debt, genes and 'superbugs'. Undogmatic but sure-footed, the style is light, explaining complex issues with easy language, illustrations and cartoons. Ideas are developed chapter by chapter, yet each one stands alone. It is an easy browse.

The Little Earth Book provides hope, with new ideas and examples of people swimming against the current, for bold ideas that work in practice. It is a book as important as it is original. Learn about the issues and join the most important debate of this century.

Did you know?

- If everyone adopted the Western lifestyle we would need five earths to support us.
- In 50 years the US has — with intensive pesticide use — doubled the amount of crops lost to pests.
- Environmental disasters have already created more than 80 MILLION refugees.

www.littleearth.co.uk

THE LITTLE FOOD BOOK

The Little Food Book
An explosive account of the food we eat today

Craig Sams

Our own livelihoods are at risk – from the food we eat. Original, stimulating, mini-essays about what is wrong with our food today, and about the greatest challenge of the new century: how to produce enough food without further damaging our health, the environment and vulnerable countries. Written by Craig Sams, Chairman of the Soil Association, it is concise, deeply informative and an important contribution to the great food debate. Just like The Little Earth Book, this is pithy, yet intellectually credible, wry yet deadly serious.

- A brilliant and easy-to-read synthesis of complex subjects
- Pertinent – food is a daily issue – organics, genetically-modified crops, farming practices, healthy eating
- Especially timely – the decline of the rural economy, foot and mouth, changes to the Common Agricultural Policy
- Compact size – an excellent gift, easy to pack.

Extracts from book:

"In the UK alone 25,000,000 kilos of pesticides are sprayed on food every year."

"In 2001 the World Trade Organisation fined the EU $120 million for suggesting that US meat imports should label the presence of hormone residues."

"Aspartame is a neurotoxin that probably causes as much brain damage as mobile phone use."

"300,000 Americans a year die of obesity."

"Research indicates that monosodium glutimate is a contributing factor in Alzheimer's disease."

"Globally, the market for organic food in 2001 exceeded $20 billion."

There is room for optimism – but you need to read this engrossing little book first!

WWW.SPECIALPLACESTOSTAY.COM

Britain

France

Ireland

Italy

Portugal

Spain...

all in one place!

On the unfathomable and often unnavigable sea of internet accommodation pages, those who have discovered **www.specialplacestostay.com** have found it to be an island of reliability. Not only will you find a database full of trustworthy, up-to-date information about all our Special Places to Stay across Europe, but also:

- Links to the web sites of all of the places from the series

- Colourful, clickable, interactive maps to help you find the right place

- The facility to make most bookings by e-mail – even if you don't have e-mail yourself

- Online purchasing of our books, securely and cheaply

- Regular, exclusive special offers on titles from the series

- The latest news about future editions, new titles and new places

The site is constantly evolving and is frequently updated, providing news, updates and special features that won't appear anywhere else but in our window on the worldwide web.

Russell Wilkinson, Web Producer
website@specialplacestostay.com

If you'd like to receive news and updates about our books by e-mail, send a message to **newsletter@specialplacestostay.com**

ORDER FORM UK

All these Special Places to Stay books, The Little Earth Book and
The Little Food Book are available in major bookshops or you may
order them direct. Post and packaging are FREE within the UK.

		Price	No. copies
French Bed & Breakfast	Edition 8	£15.99	
French Hotels, Inns and Other Places	Edition 2	£11.99	
French Holiday Homes	Edition 1	£11.99	
Paris Hotels	Edition 4	£9.99	
British Bed & Breakfast	Edition 7	£14.99	
British Hotels, Inns and Other Places	Edition 4	£12.99	
Bed & Breakfast for Garden Lovers	Edition 2	£14.99	
British Holiday Homes	Edition 1	£9.99	
London	Edition 1	£9.99	
Ireland	Edition 4	£12.99	
Spain	Edition 5	£13.99	
Portugal	Edition 2	£9.99	
Italy	Edition 2	£11.95	
The Little Earth Book	Edition 3	£6.99	
The Little Food Book	Edition 1	£6.99	
Please make cheques payable to **Alastair Sawday Publishing**	Total £		

Please send cheques to: Alastair Sawday Publishing,
The Home Farm Stables, Barrow Gurney, Bristol BS48 3RW.
For credit card orders call 01275 464891 or order directly
from our web site www.specialplacestostay.com

Title   First name

Surname

Address

Postcode

Tel

If you do not wish to receive mail from otherlike-minded companies,
please tick here ☐
If you would prefer not to receive information about special offers on our books,
please tick here ☐

ORDER FORM USA

All these books are available at your local bookstore, or you may order
direct. Allow two to three weeks for delivery.

		Price	No. copies
Spain	Edition 5	$19.95	
Ireland	Edition 4	$17.95	
French Bed & Breakfast	Edition 8	$19.95	
Paris Hotels	Edition 4	$14.95	
British Holiday Homes	Edition 1	$14.95	
British Hotels, Inns and other places	Edition 4	$17.95	
French Hotels, Inns and other places	Edition 2	$19.95	
British Bed & Breakfast	Edition 7	$19.95	
London	Edition 1	$12.95	
Italy	Edition 2	$17.95	
French Holiday Homes	Edition 1	$17.95	
	Total $		

Shipping in the continental USA: $3.95 for one book,
$4.95 for two books, $5.95 for three or more books.
Outside continental USA, call (800) 243-0495 for prices.
For delivery to AK, CA, CO, CT, FL, GA, IL, IN, KS, MI, MN, MO, NE,
NM, NC, OK, SC, TN, TX, VA, and WA, please add appropriate sales tax.

Please make checks payable to: **Total $**
The Globe Pequot Press

To order by phone with MasterCard or Visa: (800) 243-0495,
9am to 5pm EST; by fax: (800) 820-2329, 24 hours;
through our Web site: www.globe-pequot.com; or by mail:
The Globe Pequot Press, P.O. Box 480, Guilford, CT 06437

Date

Name

Address

Town

State

Zip code

Tel

Fax

REPORT FORM

Comments on existing entries and new discoveries

If you have any comments on entries in this guide, please let us have them. If you have a favourite house, hotel, inn or other new discovery, not just in Portugal, please let us know about it.

Book title: _____

Entry no: _____ Edition no: _____

New recommendation: _____

Country: _____

Name of property: _____

Address: _____

_____

_____

Postcode: _____

Tel: _____

Date of stay: _____

Comments: _____

_____

_____

From: _____

Address: _____

_____

_____

Postcode: _____

Tel: _____

Please send the completed form to:

Alastair Sawday Publishing,
The Home Farm Stables, Barrow Gurney, Bristol BS48 3RW
or go to www.specialplacestostay.com and click on 'contact'.

Thank you.

BOOKING FORM

Á Atençèo de:
To:
_____

Date:
_____

Estimado Senhor/Estimada Senhora,

Agradeciamos que efectuassem uma reserva em nome de:
Please could you make us a reservation in the name of:

_____

Para	noite(s)	Chegada a: dia	mês	ano
For	night(s)	Arriving: day	month	year
		Partida a: dia	mês	ano
		Leaving: day	month	year

Desejamos   quarto,   :
We would like   rooms, arranged as follows:

Duplo	Camos seperadas
Double bed	Twin beds
Triplo	Individual
Triple	Single
Suite	Apartamento
Suite	Appartment

Também desejamos jantar: Sim   Não Para   pesisoas
We will also be requiring   dinner yes no   for person(s)

Agradeciamos que nos enviassem confirmação desta reserva para o
endereço acima mencionado. (Pode utilizar este formulário ou uma
fotocópia do mesmo com a sua assinatura.)

Please could you send us confirmation of our reservation to the
address below (this form or a photocopy of it with your signature
could be used).

Nome: **Name:**
_____

Endereço: **Address:**
_____

_____

Tel No: E-mail:
_____

Fax No:
_____

QUICK REFERENCE INDICES

Wheelchair If you need houses which are wheelchair-friendly, contact
these owners.

Northern Portugal

• 17 •

Central Portugal

• 37 • 38 • 42 • 47 • 57 • 64 • 66 • 69 • 70 • 72 • 74 • 78 •
79 • 80 • 81

Spain

• 88 • 95 • 96 • 111 • 119 • 120 • 121 • 144

Self-catering These places are self-catering.

Northern Portugal

• 2 • 5 • 9 • 16 • 26 • 36 • 37 • 38 • 40 • 42 • 46 • 47 • 55 •
57 • 60 • 66 • 76 • 78 • 82 • 83 • 84 • 87

Southern Portugal

• 89 • 93 • 97 • 99 • 110 • 111 • 112 • 114 • 115 • 117 • 119 •
120 • 123 • 127 • 128 • 130 • 131 • 133 • 136 • 137 • 144

Bikes These owners have bikes you can borrow or can organise
local hire.

Northern Portugal

• 2 • 12 • 13 • 14 • 15 • 16 • 17 • 21 • 25 • 26 • 29 • 31 • 32

Central Portugal

• 35 • 40 • 44 • 57 • 61 • 69 • 75 • 84 • 85 • 87

Southern Portugal

• 89 • 92 • 95 • 99 • 100 • 101 • 105 • 107 • 110 • 115 • 119 •
120 • 121 • 123 • 126 • 129 • 130 • 133 • 135 • 136 •140
• 142 • 144

Walk The following places have good walks close by.

Northern Portugal

• 1 • 2 • 3 • 4 • 5 • 6 • 7 • 8 • 10 • 11 • 13 • 15 • 16 •18 •
20 • 21 • 22 • 23 • 24 • 25 • 28 • 30

QUICK REFERENCE INDICES

Central Portugal

• 34 • 35 • 36 • 38 • 39 • 40 • 43 • 44 • 47 • 49 • 50 • 52 • 53 •
56 • 57 • 58 • 59 • 60 • 61 • 62 • 63 • 65 • 67 • 74 • 76 • 78
• 79 • 80 • 81 • 82 • 84 • 85 • 86 • 87

Southern Portugal

89 • 90 • 91 • 93 • 96 • 97 • 98 • 99 • 100 • 101 • 102 • 103
• 104 •106 • 107 • 109 • 110 • 111 • 112 • 114 • 115 • 119 •
120 • 121 • 122 • 123 • 124 • 125 • 126 • 127 • 129 • 130
• 134 • 135 • 136 • 137 • 140• 143 • 144

Pool These are houses with a swimming pool in the grounds.

Northern Portugal

• 1 • 2 • 4 • 6 • 7 • 8 • 98 • 10 • 11 • 12 • 13 •14 • 15 • 16 •
21 • 23 • 24 • 25 • 26 • 27 • 28 • 29 • 30 • 31 • 32 • 33

Central Portugal

• 34 • 35 • 36 • 38 • 40 • 41 • 44 • 47 • 49 • 50 • 52 • 54 • 55 •
57 • 59 • 60 • 61 • 62 • 65 • 66 • 67 • 70 • 72 • 76 • 77 • 78
• 79 • 80 • 81 • 82 • 84 • 85 • 86 • 87

Southern Portugal

• 89 • 92 • 94 • 95 • 97 • 99 • 100 • 101 • 102 • 103 • 104 •
105 • 109 • 110 • 111 • 116 • 117 • 119 • 121 • 123 • 124
• 125 • 126 • 127 • 128 • 130 • 132 • 133 • 134 •• 135 • 136 •
137 • 138 • 139 • 140 • 141 • 142 •143 • 144

Casa Branca These houses are part of the Casa Branca group. For further
information see www.portSouthern Portugal

• 113 • 116 • 117 • 118 • 119 • 121 • 123

INDEX BY PLACE NAME

INDEX BY PLACE NAME

INDEX BY PROPERTY NAME

INDEX BY PROPERTY NAME

EXCHANGE RATE TABLE

Euro€	US$	£ Sterling
1	1.08	0.66
5	5.40	3.30
7	7.56	4.62
10	10.80	6.60
15	16.20	9.90
20	21.60	13.20
30	32.40	19.80
40	43.20	26.40
50	54.00	33.00
100	108.00	66.00
150	162.00	99.00

January 2003

EXPLANATION OF SYMBOLS

Treat each one as a guide rather than a statement of fact and check important points when booking.

Full and approved wheelchair facilities for at least one bedroom and bathroom and access to all ground-floor common areas.

Ground-floor bedrooms for people of limited mobility.

No smoking anywhere in the house.

Pets are welcome but may have to sleep in an outbuilding or your car. Check when booking.

Payment by cash or cheque only.

Credit cards accepted; most commonly Visa and Mastercard

Vegetarians catered for with advance warning. All hosts can cater for vegetarians at breakfast.

Most, but not necessarily all, ingredients are organic, organically grown, home-grown or locally grown.

Working Farm.

Childern are positively welcomed, with no age restrictions, but cots, high chairs etc are not necessarily availble.

Your hosts speak English, whether perfectly or not.

This house has pets of its own that live in the house: dog, cat, duck, parrot...

Swimming pool on the premises.

You can borrow or hire bikes.

Good hiking nearby.

Air conditioning in bedrooms. It may be a centrally-operated system or individual apparatus.

REVISED EXPLANATION OF SYMBOLS

With many apologies...

during the production of this book we made a novel error
failing to match symbol images to their correct descriptions –
below are the, sometimes incongruous but correct,
interpretations of the symbols as they appear on the property
pages. We are embarrassed by, and very sorry for, the confusion
this may cause.

Full and approved wheelchair facilities for at least one bedroom
and bathroom and access to all ground-floor common areas.

Ground-floor bedrooms for people of limited mobility.

No smoking anywhere in the house.

Pets are welcome but may have to sleep in an outbuilding
or your car. Check when booking.

Payment by cash or cheque only.

Credit cards accepted; most commonly Visa and Mastercard.

Most, but not necessarily all, ingredients are organic,
organically grown, home-grown or locally grown.

Working farm.

Children are positively welcomed, with no age restrictions,
but cots, high chairs etc are not necessarily available.

Pets live in the house: dog, cat, duck, parrot...

Swimming pool on the premises.

You can borrow or hire bikes here.

Air conditioning in bedrooms. It may be a centrally-operated
system or individual apparatus.